Building Learning Communit

How to Integrate Academic, Social, and Emotional Learning

Bernard Novick
Jeffrey S. Kress
Maurice J. Elias

Association for Supervision and Curriculum Development
Alexandria, Virginia USA

Association for Supervision and Curriculum Development
1703 N. Beauregard St. • Alexandria, VA 22311-1714 USA
Telephone: 800-933-2723 or 703-578-9600 • Fax: 703-575-5400
Web site: http://www.ascd.org • E-mail: member@ascd.org

ASCD publications present a variety of viewpoints. The views expressed or implied in this book should not be interpreted as official positions of the Association.

All Web links in this book are correct as of the publication date below but may have become inactive or otherwise modified since that time. If you notice a deactivated or changed link, please e-mail books@ascd.org with the words "Link Update" in the subject line. In your message, please specify the Web link, the book title, and the page number on which the link appears.

Printed in the United States of America.

s8/2002
ASCD Product No. 101240
ASCD member price: $18.95   nonmember price: $22.95

Library of Congress Cataloging-in-Publication Data
Novick, Bernard, 1933-1999
  Building learning communities with character : how to integrate
academic, social, and emotional learning / Bernard Novick, Jeffrey S.
Kress, and Maurice J. Elias.
      p. cm.
Includes bibliographical references and index.
  ISBN 0-87120-665-X (alk. paper)
 1. Affective education. 2. Social learning. 3. Character—Study and
teaching. I. Kress, Jeffrey S. II. Elias, Maurice J. III. Title.
  LB1072 .N68 2002
  370.15'3--dc21

                              2002006644

08 07 06 05 04 03 02   10 9 8 7 6 5 4 3 2 1

Building Learning Communities with Character
How to Integrate Academic, Social, and Emotional Learning

Acknowledgments

During the writing of this book, we drew on our experiences in schools with innovative, forward-thinking administrators who excel in implementing programs while simultaneously embodying the character and value traits they want in their students. The list of these administrators is quite lengthy. Here, we mention a few administrators with whom we have worked closely, acknowledging their efforts as well as their influence on our thinking: Tom Schuyler, Larry Leverett, Carole Beris, Frank Fehn, Jacqueline Norris, Tony Bencivenga, Richard Kuder, Bruce Ellinger, Theresa O'Donnell, Ray Pasi, Virginia Brinson, Joseph Ierardi, Gene Vescia, Mario Barbiere, Phyllis Catz, and Marjorie Heller. Also, we thank our colleagues at the Social Decision Making/Social Problem Solving program in New Brunswick, New Jersey, particularly Tom Schuyler, Linda Bruene, and Erin Bruno.

In addition, Jeffrey Kress would like to thank his wife Adena; his son Ezra; his parents, June and Sidney Kress; and his colleagues at the Davidson School and the Department of Jewish Education at the Jewish Theological Seminary, particularly Dr. Aryeh Davidson. Maurice Elias would like to thank his wife, Ellen, and daughters, Sara Elizabeth and Samara Alexandra. Further, he acknowledges his colleagues at the Collaborative for Academic, Social, and Emotional Learning (www.casel.org), with whom he is studying implementation practices that facilitate excellence in both the cognitive and social-emotional realms.

This book is imbued with the spirit and wisdom of Bernie Novick and could not have been completed without the support and assistance of his life partner, Phyllis Novick, herself a gifted guidance counselor.

Finally, we would like to thank those at the Association for Supervision and Curriculum Development who helped make this book a reality: Julie Houtz, Nancy Modrak, John O'Neil, Stephanie Selice, Marge Scherer, and Tim Sniffin. Their dedication to excellence in both the content and visual form of their books is inspiring.

Preface

Social and emotional learning and character education are complementary approaches to strengthening a person's ability to understand, manage, and express the social and emotional aspects of life and to organize action in a positive, goal-directed manner. For children, social-emotional learning and character education underpin their ability to successfully manage the tasks of everyday life such as learning, forming relationships, solving everyday problems, and adapting to the complex demands of growth and development. We feel these approaches greatly help school administrators improve the quality of student and staff learning and the climate of their schools.

This book is designed for administrators at any level of experience with social-emotional and character education programs. It is intended for people with little or no prior background in these programs or related areas; for people with some knowledge, but need help in introducing the programs to their school; and for people who may have begun the implementation process, but want additional ideas to increase the chance of success. Interest in social-emotional learning and character education is growing, and many administrators have been exposed to ideas from a variety of sources. These include popular books (e.g., Daniel Goleman's *Emotional Intelligence*, 1995), magazine articles, and journals targeting administrators (Elias, Zins, Weissberg, & Associates, 1997; *Educational Leadership* Special Issue, May, 1997), and media-based staff development tools (National Center for Innovation and Education, 1999). Appendix A provides a basic overview of social-emotional learning.

Differences in terminology should not mask similar perspectives. Whether you are familiar with "social and emotional learning," "emotional intelligence/EQ," "social competence," or some other term, the underlying concepts are greatly similar. Schools, for example, frequently discuss character education as a concern. In fact, our home state of New Jersey recently set aside funding to implement character education programs in each of its districts. However, as with many efforts, more attention has been paid to what a program is called rather than how to effectively introduce it. In our experience, social-emotional and character education approaches overlap greatly (see Appendix B). In addition, it is clearly much easier to have good intentions than good programming, regardless of the terminology. This guide will help you avoid the pitfalls of piecemeal, "magic bullet" programming and find the pathways and processes that help create sustainable and renewable approaches.

For simplicity of language, we wrote this book from the school, rather than district, perspective. However, the principles and strategies presented are derived from our work with entire districts as well as individual schools, and they can be applied at this broader level. Where special considerations occur with regard to working at a district level, we mention those explicitly.

How to Use This Book

The book is organized around a problem-solving approach. After an overview chapter, the book continues with a discussion on readiness. The chapters following devote themselves to eight steps of a particular problem-solving model we have used in schools for more than two decades. A problem-solving model fits the task of implementing social-emotional programs very well, because it represents a determination to succeed in a systematic manner that addresses issues and overcomes obstacles. Administrators work effectively with problem-solving approaches, and this is another example of how one model has been applied effectively in the context of social-emotional learning and character education. The concluding chapter addresses how to sustain success after a program is established.

Each chapter begins with an overview of the step being covered and its specific usefulness. The bulk of each chapter is devoted to guidelines, activities, frameworks, rating scales, surveys, and other tools to facilitate implementation.

At the end of each chapter, there is a section called "Transitions: Review and a Look Ahead." Here, you have an opportunity to review key points and to personalize the ideas of each chapter through a series of brief questions or reflections about how the material applies to your school or district.

We strongly urge you to maintain a designated notebook, perhaps on your computer, to record the results of your ideas, suggestions, and reflections. Such a notebook also provides a place to keep track of what other schools and districts are doing in the social-emotional and character education area—something we also emphasize. Networking with others who travel down a similar road, whether or not they use the same procedures, is an additional crucial part of this endeavor.

The process presented in this book has led to many successes. Combined with the important elements of your own ideas and suggestions as well as what you learn from networking, it can eventually create the kind of synergy of social, emotional, and academic skills that characterize our most effective schools.

An Overview of Themes in Social-Emotional Learning and Character Education

Students today differ from those of a decade or two ago. They are products of a different era and different socialization patterns. Despite relatively greater material advantages when compared to earlier generations, students today are also more emotionally and behaviorally troubled, more depressed, more stressed, and less ready to learn in-depth.

Thus, work on social-emotional learning and character education occurs against the backdrop of too many incidents of actual or, more often, threatened school violence and other problem behavior. After a shooting in Santana High School in San Diego, the principal told CNN, "This is my worst nightmare." Nightmare is an apt word. Until education in character and social-emotional skills takes its place alongside education in reading and math, having a hit-or-miss program—or even a series of approaches—is like having an electrical circuit that is only 99.9 percent complete. Darkness results, and administrators will lament about even more nightmares. These nightmares may not have the degree of tragedy seen in San Diego or at Columbine High School in Colorado, but smaller incidents do their share to damage the educational process and erode the fabric of trust among students, staff, school, and community.

We designed this book to help you—a concerned educational leader of your school and district—create that closed circuit and generate the light of learning instead of the darkness of violence, disaffection, and disillusionment. When you provide students with the tools they need for sound character and social-emotional growth to accompany their academic skills, you give them life gifts that elevate their minds, hearts, and spirits and positively affect all those with whom these students come in contact. This goal requires an approach to social-emotional issues that incorporates entire schools, coordinates with other elements of schooling, continues across all grade levels, and builds to a point of success and satisfaction over multiple years.

Emotional Intelligence

Daniel Goleman's 1995 book, *Emotional Intelligence*, galvanized public interest in social and emotional skills in the classroom and beyond. Goleman gathered research from numerous fields, particularly cognitive neuroscience, to confirm what many teachers and administrators had learned through years of observation and experience: Students' efforts to learn often run up against formidable interference from a myriad of social and emotional factors. Students bring some of these factors from home to school, and others are picked up during the school day.

Goleman wrote a follow-up to his original work, titled *Working with Emotional Intelligence* (1998), where he continued his argument for the centrality of social and emotional skills and expanded his review of research to cover the predictive strength of such skills for success in the workplace. Not surprisingly, the array of competencies important to students in their social and school experiences is also vital to successful workplace functioning.

Goleman describes emotional intelligence as consisting of five areas (see Appendix A for further elaboration of social-emotional learning concepts):

1. Self-awareness—recognizing feelings as they occur in real-life situations.

2. Managing emotions—coping with strong feelings so you are not overwhelmed and paralyzed by them.

3. Self-motivation—being goal-oriented and able to channel emotions toward desired outcomes.

4. Empathy and perspective-taking—recognizing emotions in others and understanding others' points of view.

5. Social skills—handling social relationships effectively.

Promoting Social and Emotional Learning: Guidelines for Educators (Elias et al., 1997) builds on these concepts. The book, cowritten by one this book's authors, brings the work of Goleman and others to bear on specific issues in program planning and implementation. To do this, it defines a comprehensive approach to addressing social-emotional learning, which includes the following domains:

1. Establish a school climate articulating specific themes, character elements, or values. Schools must stand for something in the minds and hearts of everyone who spends time in them. So much is thrown at staff and students alike that without some coherent organizing principles or cognitive "hooks" to organize or hang onto the various items, most information will fall away. Further, schools must send a message about character: about how students should conduct themselves as learners, how staff should conduct themselves as educators, and how others who work in schools, including parents, should conduct themselves as supporters of learning. Ideally, schools establishing such climates work within districts that have incorporated social-emotional and character programs into their overall mission statements or board policies.

2. Increase explicit instruction in social-emotional skills. If you and your staff want students to learn and internalize the general skills needed to negotiate complex interactions in school, the workplace, and life (e.g., self-control, listening, communication, problem solving), then you also must have a plan to reach that goal. Social-emotional learning and character theory strongly suggests explicit instruction across grade levels is necessary for students to achieve the depth of learning required for them to apply those kinds of skills without prompting.

3. Increase explicit instruction in health-promotion and problem-prevention skills. Evidence clearly shows generic social-emotional life skills do not transfer well to specific areas, such as premature sexual behavior and smoking, drug, and alcohol use. Further, those skills do not help students much in figuring out how to develop a healthy lifestyle, including patterns of diet, exercise, and sleep. Therefore, to help your students acquire the health-promotion and problem-prevention skills they need to be good learners and citizens of your school, you need to provide them with context-specific instruction in the application of social-emotional life skills (e.g., how to use assertive communication to refuse drugs when offered).

4. Set up systems to enhance coping skills and social support for transitions, crises, and resolving conflicts.

In many schools, students' ability to access resources is related to the severity of problems they experience. But schools need to set up services for students before they experience personal or familial life crises, life transitions, or other situations. Extra support could help to forestall or minimize the potential problems caused by these situations. Guidance counselors advocate this point of view, which is consistent with the emerging field of professional school counseling. Similarly, because students certainly are going to encounter interpersonal conflicts, they would benefit from instruction in conflict resolution as a standard part of their school program, rather than after they encounter difficulties.

5. Create widespread, systematic opportunities for positive, contributory service. Positive, contributory service experiences, carried out in a pedagogically sound manner, provide students with a chance to build meaningful relationships that provide a sense of usefulness and purpose. In addition to creating a positive bond to school and community, service experiences, which can begin in elementary school, allow students to feel part of a greater whole and to develop an increased sense of empathy and social concern.

As a school administrator, you face social-emotional and character issues on a variety of levels. First, as an instructional leader, you may want to review the five domains and consider what you may already be doing. For example, your school already may implement programs that either include social-emotional skills instruction as a major focus (such as life skills or interpersonal problem-solving or conflict-resolution programs), or incorporate these skills as a way to approach a variety of problems in and out of the school environment (e.g., substance abuse prevention or conflict resolution). Second, as a manager, you involve yourself in the social and emotional functioning of your staff. You address this role implicitly and explicitly in part through your attitude and approach in dealing with staff (e.g., adapting a supportive, rather than critical, role during staff evaluations), or through more direct intervention (e.g., helping to mediate a dispute between coworkers). Finally, as a person, you must deal with your own social and emotional issues. These play out in your interactions with staff, other administrators, board members, parents, students, community residents, and others. And balancing the requirements of your own family and work life may well represent the most challenging—and important—application of social and emotional skills.

Key Elements in Creating Sustained Change

Many activities in the educational marketplace promise great improvements in your school and for your students—like an educational "cheese of the month" club. Unfortunately, the old adage "the more things change, the more they remain the same" keeps proving itself right. You have no doubt read about how institutional change *can* lead to genuine differences in the climate, tone, and productivity in schools. This book draws on the authors' direct experiences with work focusing on sustained, long-term change.

There are two key elements in sustained change, particularly in the area of social-emotional learning and character education:

1. Developing a problem-solving and management-planning process to install a social-emotional learning program.
2. Harnessing specific insights based on work in schools that have successfully installed and sustained these programs.

As an administrator, you are constantly asked to take certain actions because another school system has done so and is claiming success; because the literature is full of articles on a topic; or because an important person likes a particular program or approach. The resulting revolving door is draining on staff and rarely accomplishes its purpose.

Answers mean little to a person who does not understand or accept the question's validity. Solving a problem requires caring about the issue in question and finding a process for addressing it. That process begins with recognizing and framing an issue or problem of concern, buying into it, and wanting to solve it—not applying a Band-Aid or mollifying a political constituency.

Evidence from Experience and Research

The most successful schools and organizations are adaptive. Their staff members have a clear sense of the organization's function or purpose and are willing to change its form or structure in response to environmental factors or outcomes that indicate the need for modification. In order to be adaptive and know when and what to change, leaders need to understand the form or structure of their schools and have a model that is clear and useful. Just as students may be confused by the assortment of social and behavioral interventions targeted at them, administrators may also become victims of good intentions. Administrators must answer to multiple constituencies, who may not share common goals, and face a variety of models for change. An organizing framework is as vital for the process of planning social-emotional programming as it is for the content of the program.

A nine-step decision-making and problem-solving process forms the core of this book. It is based on a social problem-solving approach developed by such researchers as George Spivack and Myrna Shure (1974), Roger Weissberg and Mark Greenberg (1997), and this book's coauthor Maurice Elias (with John Clabby, 1986; with Steven Tobias, 1996). Figure 1.1 summarizes this problem-solving process and highlights how each step can be applied to the process of implementing social-emotional learning and character education. This approach, similar in many ways to what is often referred to as "action-research," also serves as the framework for moving from plans to action. Like the model we present here, action-research provides an ongoing and systematic approach in which program implementation and ongoing program modification and improvement come together in a cycle of problem definition, goal setting, solution generating and implementation, and outcome evaluation (see Appendix C).

Figure 1.1
An Eight-Step Social Decision-Making and
Social Problem-Solving Approach

Problem Solving Step 1
Recognize feelings: know when to start problem solving

Problem Solving Step 2
Identify problems: look at the current situation

Problem Solving Step 3
Set goals: focus the change efforts

Problem Solving Step 4
Generate options: think of many things to do

Problem Solving Step 5
Envision outcomes: consider all the consequences

Problem Solving Step 6
Choose carefully: select a goal-oriented or goal-driven solution

Problem Solving Step 7
Plan prescriptively: anticipate all details and roadblocks

Problem Solving Step 8
Learn constantly: obtain feedback and modify accordingly

What Is the Process Outlined by These Steps?

Strong emotions you detect in yourself or in others are often the most reliable signs that there may be a problem in your organization. Feelings serve as an important cue for you to pursue a problem-solving process.

Your next task is to face your present circumstances realistically. This may sound simple, but a moment's honest reflection will confirm that facing reality is quite difficult. As specifically as you can, put problems into words. You should avoid placing blame; regardless of their cause, you must identify problems clearly and constructively.

Once you can put problems into words, you can begin to set goals. Well-formulated goals are realistic, attainable, under your control, and of preeminent importance. If you consider feelings as catalysts for action, then regard goals as driving forces and guardrails while action moves ahead.

Brainstorming is the process of creating alternative pathways. You must be open to any possible ideas from many sources. Editing comes later. Brainstorming results in better outcomes, and it improves your process because you can respond to critics and to supporters of unused ideas by showing the range of options you examined before advocating a course of action.

Each option you generate has many consequences—short and long term, positive and negative, direct and indirect—and many implications. You must carefully envision what will result for each possible path you can choose.

When it comes time to make a choice, the best solution for your situation is one that reaches *your* goals. It is not the "ideal" solution, because one does not exist.

We are not at the end of the process, however; you must check for feasibility. Just as you envision consequences to various pathways, you also must envision each path in detail. Planning is not a flawless process; pathways are not perfectly predictable. But if you cannot even envision going from your starting point to your destination, you may want to reconsider your options and find another path. Planning is a critical step in the process of creating sustained change and is the strength of truly effective leaders. Involve as many constituents as possible, plan the path you will take as realistically and specifically as you can, and predict pitfalls and how they will be addressed. If the course of action still looks feasible, pursue it.

Although you may prefer a process of "Ready! Aim! Fire!", your own experience will tell you that you may need to modify it to "Ready! Fire! Aim!" Because no plan is perfect, you must find ways to keep track of what is happening and reconsider what you will do in light of what you learn. You engage in an ongoing action-research cycle, and this requires you to always check for results while you are implementing your plans. Social-emotional and character activities, like any other innovation brought into a school to solve a problem and reach a goal, must be monitored to keep them on target and be modified as conditions warrant.

The following chapters take a more detailed look at each step in the problem-solving process and elaborate the management and planning activities that will help you use this process to bring social-emotional learning and character education to your school in a lasting and powerful way.

▼   ▼   ▼

Transitions: Review and a Look Ahead

Too often, schools become locked into patterns of exhausting, hectic, and seemingly endless activity without time to reconsider its meaning. One contribution of emotional intelligence theory is that time for reflection is a necessity, especially as a precursor to bringing comprehensive social-emotional programs to your school. Therefore, in this and all succeeding chapters, you will find a *review* of key points, a *bridge* to the following chapter, and an opportunity for you to consider some questions designed to prompt *reflections for action* on your part. These questions are designed to help you sort out and organize the many emotions and thoughts evoked while you read this book and apply it to your organization.

Review

- For today's student in today's societal context, social-emotional learning and character education is essential for social and academic success.
- Sound character is based on a set of social-emotional skills that allows children to enact that character, and these skills must be developed at multiple levels and in a systematic and sustained manner.
- A problem-solving approach to planning and managing innovations in schools is most effective for long-term success, especially when the process is carried out in a collaborative and socially and emotionally sensitive way.
- Creating enduring change requires an ongoing, goal-focused, action-research approach to adapting to changing circumstances.

Bridge

Social-emotional learning and character education have been a concern of many educators, but their place often is unclear. Mounting evidence shows effective schools address these programs alongside academics, resulting in positive synergy in both areas and a school that is a vibrant place to learn and work. Yet, as an administrator, you know bringing any lasting change to schools is a challenge. Chapter 2 includes some important issues that you must consider before beginning in earnest, to ensure that you and your staff are on the right road and ready to put your energies into a process that has a substantial chance to succeed.

Reflections for Action

- What are you particularly proud of in your school that you want to enhance or share?
- How satisfied are you and your staff with the practices or outcomes of education in your school?
- What is your view of the climate or culture of the school?
- Are otherwise smart people—staff or students—not doing good work?
- Do interpersonal conflicts among and between adults and students lead otherwise promising projects to fail?
- What helps to provide a unifying feeling that makes a team out of the various individuals in your school?
- How are all students being equipped with the skills they need for lives of continuous learning and contribution?
- How has your school come to its current social-emotional practices or programs?
- To what extent do you know what schools similar to yours do with regard to similar programs?

Readiness:
Assess Your School's Potential for Change

As an administrator starting a process to bring change to your school, you no doubt have faced advice to avoid rocking the boat. Your willingness to address social and emotional concerns in your school is a vital first step, but one that should be taken with eyes wide open. The more you think about the potential of your organization's members to participate in the change process, the fewer surprises you find as the process unfolds.

Readiness for change does not require at the outset equally strong beliefs and commitments to change on everyone's part. However, it does require that you, as a leader in your school or district, can envision the majority of your staff eventually coming on board.

Three Guiding Beliefs

The National Center for Innovation and Education (1999) set three guiding beliefs as the core of most social and emotional learning programs. These beliefs are "the missing piece" in educational reform and change (Elias et al., 1997). A set of focused and linked recollections follows each belief. Review the following to see the nature and strength of your own beliefs.

    1. Caring relationships form the foundation for learning. Think of situations where you learned the most. How often did these situations involve a relationship with someone who fostered that learning? Can you recall relationships with mentors, supervisors, or other instructors where the caring nature of that bond was essential to your internalizing what you learned?

    2. Emotions affect how learning takes place and what is learned. How well do you work, learn, or perform when you are deeply worried about a personal matter? Highly angry over something that happened earlier in the day? Afraid about what awaits you later? Depressed because you anticipate failure?

    3. Goal setting and problem solving provide direction and energy for learning. How well do you solve problems when you are unsure what the problem really is or what goal you are trying to achieve? To what extent have you found your stress relates to a lack of clear goals or priorities?

Apply the same sets of reflections to your staff and students. Where do they learn best, how do strong emotions affect their work, and how do they respond to clear goals, a defined problem, or a lack thereof? If you conclude that there is consensus among your staff, students, and yourself on the importance of the three guiding beliefs, you are likely ready for the voyage to bring social-emotional learning and character education into your schools.

Trust Allows Change to Occur

If you are uncertain about proceeding because you are not sure to what degree your staff members share the guiding beliefs, consider another key dimension—trust. Trust is essential within a staff, among students, between staff and students, and, of course, where the administration is involved. Trust allows people to proceed on a path of change even though precise directions might not be clear. Trust allows staff members to follow strong, concerned, and respectful leadership, even when they are not completely sure they share a particular ideological commitment.

Why? Ultimately, caring relationships form the foundation for learning. Trust is a powerful developmental process that works with staff the way trust in caregivers allows toddlers to venture farther and farther out into the world. Without doubt, you formulate your own ideas about what builds trust in relationships, in groups, within classrooms, among faculty members, and within school buildings. The presence of these trust-building elements makes a school receptive to innovations, including social-emotional programs.

In summary, a set of shared beliefs about the importance of social-emotional learning and character education—coupled with a strong need for change or sense of mutual trust—signals that potentially fertile ground exists for efforts to begin. Readiness for change, however, is a blend of willingness and capacity. Any organization's future functioning is related to its current status. A realistic look at the way your setting operates can help you prepare for change.

Audit of Organizational Culture

As a way to begin understanding the culture of your school, use the questions in Figure 2.1 to review your organization in terms of its readiness to change. Schools can't just change how and when administrators want them to, no matter how enlightened, committed, or driven educational leaders might be. There is a history that cannot be erased, and people do not easily or quickly give up habits and work patterns.

Figure 2.1
Readiness for Change

Would you consider your school to be more...

    Autocratic   ————OR————   Democratic

Is the normal pattern of action to...

    Follow routine   ————OR————   Take risks

When matters require some review and study, is the emphasis on a process that is...

    On time and fast   ————OR————   Deliberate

Do staff members perceive themselves to be most valued when they...

    Work as individuals   ————OR————   Work as part of a team

Is there a sense that the best staff members are those who usually...

    Follow procedures   ————OR————   Strive for excellence

Does the functioning of the school tend to reflect a view that...

    Each task or activity   ————OR————   All tasks and activities
    is independent   are related to each other and to school goals

Items in the right-hand column represent readiness trends that may be more conducive to bringing about change in your organization.

Although not necessarily polar opposites, the items in Figure 2.1 represent competing trends often encountered in school functioning. The more your school reflects the trends on the right-hand side of the table, the more conducive your school atmosphere will be to help administrators, staff, and students bring about effective change. The presence of such norms as teamwork and a commitment to excellence in the organizational culture are among the "levers" that administrators can use to mobilize and follow through on a change process. As you consider your organizational culture, try not to think of how you would like it to be, but how it is now. As a second step in your review, think about how your answers could be different if you were thinking about how you *want* your setting to function. Those areas that have the largest gaps between current and ideal status need attention because they suggest places most likely to impede readiness for change.

Understanding how the beliefs and actions of your organization may foster or inhibit change is useful as you embark on the change process. Organizational experts have identified characteristics of organizations of all kinds that are considered successful, represent excellence, and are known as "hands-on." Beliefs or actions can help define these characteristics. The work of Deal and Kennedy (1982) in this area provides valuable guidelines for determining the beliefs and action patterns of your organization. Clearly, these guidelines sometimes overlap. Some administrators, however, find it easier to think of schools in terms of beliefs or action patterns, as summarized in Figure 2.2, so you should use whatever provides you with a better perspective to grasp the stronger and weaker aspects of your school culture.

Figure 2.2
Organizational Beliefs and Action Patterns

Organizational Beliefs

Would you say that the culture of your school reflects a belief

___ in the importance of enjoying one's work?

___ in being the best?

___ that people should innovate and take risks without feeling they will be punished if they fail?

___ in the importance of attending to details?

___ in the importance of people as individuals?

___ in superior quality and service?

___ in the importance of continuous educational growth?

___ in the importance of informality to improve the flow of communication?

___ in the importance of "hands-on" management and the notion that supervisors at all levels should be active, take initiative, and "walk the talk"?

___ in the importance of a recognized organizational philosophy supported by those at the top?

Organizational Action Patterns

In your school, to what extent do staff members at all levels

___ share a management philosophy?

___ emphasize the importance of people to the success of the organization?

___ encourage rituals and ceremonies to celebrate school events?

___ identify successful people and sing their praises?

___ communicate the culture, especially to newcomers?

___ follow a common set of informal rules of behavior?

___ articulate a strong, clear set of values?

___ set and monitor high standards for performance?

___ identify with and exemplify a definitive school character?

Implications for Practice

When you are contemplating bringing character education or similar programs to a school, understanding the aspects of your organization described in Figure 2.2 provides you with essential background. The audit of organizational culture is, in a sense, about the extent to which a school already functions with a sense of positive character and with emotional intelligence. But if you find that few of the items on Figure 2.2 characterize your school, this is not necessarily a "red light" for implementing change. Think of it more as a "yellow light" suggesting slow, cautious movement. In fact, addressing any of the items related to beliefs or actions can serve as a first step toward cultural change. For example, you may find that identifying and praising good work by your employees rarely occurs. A modest jumping-off point for implementing change in this case may be to introduce positive recognition into your everyday routine. Others include ensuring administrators "walk the talk" more visibly and holding staff discussions to clarify or reaffirm organizational beliefs, values, commitment to excellence, and willingness to innovate.

The Challenge of Change

Regardless of where your organization falls on the continua suggested by the audit, implementing change always calls for proceeding with caution. Areas of strength that you have identified indicate your organization has at least some internal supports for handling the ups and downs that are par for the course in any change process. In child-centered schools where there is a commitment to excellence, educators often have surprisingly positive responses to change. Many of these educators, who have concerns about the behavior and character of their students, *want* to hear about how social-emotional learning and character education might put the school on a more positive path. School staff know intuitively that change in one area can have unanticipated outcomes in other areas. Your task as an educational leader is to show how the process of bringing in the social-emotional approach is not random or harmful, but is likely to reinforce important, positive elements of the organizational culture and help reach cherished goals for all students.

▼ ▼ ▼

Transitions: Review and a Look Ahead

Review

• You and your staff's commitment to the guiding beliefs of social-emotional learning and character education signals readiness for change.

• An audit of your organization's culture, beliefs, and actions can illuminate areas of strength and weakness that will influence the change process.

• The process of change best unfolds with clear plans and caution, particularly when there are few areas of organizational strength.

• Mutual trust between you and your staff will greatly assist the change process.

Bridge

Assessing readiness for change avoids many potential pitfalls and inappropriate starting points. This book places particular focus on identifying and working with strengths, and you are likely to become more aware of assets in your school than you were before. This understanding will help you considerably as you plan to bring social-emotional learning and character education into your school. But often, the need for change cannot wait until a school is optimally ready; sometimes it is thrust upon you by local or state mandate. Creating change is always an emotionally challenging process, and working with social-emotional and character programs is no exception. That's why the decision-making and problem-solving tools used in this book begins with a focus on feelings. Strong feelings accompany change, and you can use Chapter 3 as a guide to identify, navigate, and constructively harness the emotions involved in bringing this new approach to your school.

Reflections for Action

• How deep is your commitment to the three guiding beliefs of social-emotional learning? How have you come to feel as you do about each of these beliefs?

• How strongly do you feel your staff holds each of the guiding beliefs? Where among your staff are the beliefs strongest? Weakest?

• What strengths exist in your organization that will help in the process of systematic change?

• Which aspects of your school's culture might impede change?

• What do you want to do next to improve the prospects of social emotional approaches taking place more systematically in your setting?

Recognize Feelings:
Know When to Start Problem Solving

Negative or uncomfortable feelings can provide us with a warning or signal that something requires our attention, examination, and action. They serve as our cues to start a process of problem solving and decision making. This book is organized around a particular eight-step process found effective in more than three decades of application across every type of school and district (see Figure 3.1).

Unlike most problem-solving processes, however, the model in this book starts with emotions. Too often, descriptions of problems are sterile and devoid of people's feelings. But if they truly are problems and the organization needs to address them in a serious way, the problems are likely generating strong emotions. Uncovering and labeling feelings thus become essential for accurately defining a problem.

How to Find Out What Problems Exist

The first step in problem solving is recognizing that a problem exists. Whereas your own feelings regarding the functioning of your school are important, as an administrator, you need to supplement these views with those of other stakeholders in the school. Staff members undoubtedly make you aware—formally or informally—of their feelings about the school and their place in it. Perhaps you overhear their conversations, which can be characterized by a particular feeling or tone. You may pick up cues from faculty meetings, the teachers' room, and small group meetings you attend or hear about. As you see your students walk through the halls, what feelings can you recognize in their facial expressions and tones of voice? What are the reactions of guests in your building? Taking walking tours can be useful for gathering some of this information (Figure 3.1).

Walks around the school tend to uncover feelings that serve as catalysts for bringing social-emotional and character initiatives into schools. Walking tours might give you the following clues:

- You have a sense that the school climate is not as safe or as inclusive as desired.

Figure 3.1
A Feelings Walking Tour

Take a walk through your school building. Look in on classes, lunch and recess times, meetings, extracurricular activities, after-school and evening events—the gamut of what occurs on regular school days. Be aware of your feelings at different destinations on your tour. Where do you experience positive emotions such as pride, joy, and excitement? Where do you experience negative emotions such as anxiety, frustration, and anger? Where do you experience both types of emotions? What is triggering these emotions at these times and places?

- You feel frustrated because aspects of the school you are particularly proud of are unnoticed, unappreciated, or too limited; and you want to enhance them or share them more widely.
- You are aware of vague or specific discomfort with the directions of the school, its character, values, cohesion, or the way students act, particularly when not under close adult supervision.
- You hear staff, students, or members of the community express dissatisfaction with the practices or outcomes of education in your school.

Sometimes, to figure out the sum total of feelings you detect, you must take a step back, examine the emotions, and sort them out. You may find it helpful to use a broad working list, such as the one in Figure 3.2. Focus on feelings that predominate over two weeks or so. Differentiate between those you experience and those you become aware of in your staff and students, and note where these feelings converge. Positive feelings indicate areas of strengths; negative emotions are red flags that problems may exist. (Regular reflection of this kind serves as a useful barometer of the emotional tone of a school or other organizational unit.)

The Importance of Emotion

Emphasizing emotions represents sound practice and sound science. Biologists and neuroscientists have made great advances in understanding the biology and physiology of emotions. Emotions appear to be part of the way in which human memory is organized; they are inextricably linked with the cognitive processes for any event experienced. The way in which people remember events during a school day (including classroom instruction and faculty meetings) and access these memories for future use is linked to the emotions experienced during and surrounding those events

Figure 3.2
Feelings Experienced by School Administrators

upset	adrift	rootless	competitive
unmotivated	unsupported	overwhelmed	unappreciated
frustrated	excited	uneasy	angry
conflicted	outcast	indecisive	ignorant
resistant	resisted	in a rut	proud
enthusiastic	optimistic	motivated	despair
supported	connected	fulfilled	peaceful

(Sylwester, 1995). Memories—and therefore information—tinged with strong negative tones are the ones we are least likely to recall, dwell on, or use. Also, neural linkages may cause strong emotional reactions to have a quick and direct effect on our behavior, too fast even for cognitive processing; we may act on our emotions before we have time to think about them (Salovey & Sluyter, 1997).

From even this cursory overview, it is clear why it is so important for you to take the emotional reactions of the various citizens of your school seriously. Emotions, rather than being seen as obstacles, are part of the process for solving problems; they are the first signs something is amiss. Although we present the problem-solving process here as sequential to help you carry out a planning procedure and an action plan, the actuality is nonlinear and recursive. Feelings come into play throughout the problem-solving process, and changes in your feelings and those of your staff and students will be evident as you move through the programming steps discussed in this book. Such changes are also good cues to review your progress and see if something needs modification or affirmation.

What Do Feelings Signal?

If emotions are warning signals, it is natural to wonder what exactly they are signaling. How can you use staff members' expressions of certain feelings as clues to what they are experiencing in their personal and professional lives? Emotion researchers, such as Richard Lazarus (1999) and Paul Ekman and Richard Davidson (1994), have provided some basis for speculating about what the presence of certain emotions—either in you, your staff, or student groups—might mean:

- **Anger.** An individual—something or someone that person values greatly—has been put down, diminished, demeaned, or insulted.
- **Anxiety.** A perception of uncertainty and a threat to one's status, comfort, or physical well-being.
- **Guilt.** An important rule was broken, or there was a failure to live up to an important value, especially one held by others whom one respects or cares about greatly.
- **Shame.** Someone has failed to be the kind of person he or she wants to be, or did something or had something done to him or her that leads to a view of self that is much less than was ever imagined.
- **Deception.** A feeling of foolishness and betrayal because someone who was trusted told a lie and it was believed, leading to self-doubt as well as doubt about that other person's sincerity and trustworthiness.
- **Sadness.** An experience of an irrevocable, lasting loss.
- **Depression.** A constant sense of heaviness, joylessness, and hopelessness about the present and future.
- **Envy.** Wanting very badly what someone else has.
- **Disgust.** Having been involved with or close to an object, idea, or situation that is absolutely foreign to one's sense of one's self and what is acceptable for decent people to do.

- **Pride.** Feeling like a valued person because of involvement with an achievement, either one's own or that of a person or group with whom one strongly identifies.
- **Relief.** A sense that a distressing condition or situation has changed for the better or gone away.
- **Hope.** Looking to the future and thinking better things will take place, even if it does not look objectively that this is the case.

Schools, and the people in them, are filled with emotions. Being able to sort out strong emotions is an essential social-emotional skill and a hallmark of sound character. Strong emotions provide energy and direction to the actions of individuals, groups, and even entire schools or districts. A passion for lifelong learning is, most basically, a passion. A safe and caring school can be a rhetorical statement or a statement of how staff, students, and others entering and remaining in a building should feel the vast majority of the time.

Bringing in or expanding social-emotional and character initiatives in your school involves building everyone's capacity to recognize and appropriately act on emotions. As mentioned earlier, you can enable change by expanding a school's strengths and areas of pride, as well as focusing on areas viewed as problematic. Understanding emotions in the context of what is happening in your school allows you to set proper directions for changes to come.

▼ ▼ ▼

Transitions: Review and a Look Ahead

Review

- Negative emotions experienced by you, your staff, and your students signal that problems exist.

- Positive emotions experienced by you, your staff, and your students indicate strengths in your school.
- It is important to assess your feelings at different locations in your site and at different points throughout the change process.
- By understanding the meaning of certain emotions, you can better respond to your staff's concerns and move the change process ahead.

Bridge

Without doubt, the change process requires a high degree of emotional sensitivity on the part of anyone intending to prepare a school to improve its social-emotional efforts. Being able to use your feelings and those of others as indicators of personal or interpersonal issues includes deciphering discrepancies between what people seem to be saying and what they are displaying. Emotion researchers agree that the feelings people show in their nonverbal behavior—tone of voice, body posture, and facial expressions in particular—are harder to monitor and tend to be more "genuine" than spoken words. You will need the skill of discerning what is happening with coworkers, staff, and yourself "below the surface" when it comes to working in groups, running meetings, assigning tasks, and organizing to take on social-emotional and character initiatives. Moving ahead requires you to communicate the directions indicated by the various feelings you have identified. That is the next step in the problem-solving process.

Reflections for Action

- What feelings are most likely to serve as catalysts for action in your setting?
- What are the most common positive feelings you experience during the course of your work? When, where, and with whom do you experience these feelings?
- What are the most common negative feelings you experience during the course of your work? When, where, and with whom do you experience these feelings?

• What did you learn from your "feelings" walking tour? How has it helped you link feelings to what they might signal?

• Among the many feelings you detected, both positive and negative, which seem most important as you prepare to bring social-emotional programs into your setting more systematically?

▲   ▲   ▲

Identify Problems:
Look at the Current Situation

Present circumstances in your school must be faced realistically. This involves putting feelings into words as *problem statements*. Placing a concern, issue, or a problematic situation into explicit terms makes it much more likely that effective and focused action will follow. It does not preclude "gut reactions"; rather, it helps refine what you are reacting to. This is also the middle step—after understanding feelings—in preparing for action planning by setting realistic and feasible goals. Remember, avoid placing blame when identifying problems; regardless of their cause, you must address them effectively and constructively.

After many years of conducting social-emotional and character initiatives, implementers found upset feelings often are linked to particular sets of problems. See if any of these feelings resonate with the ones you noted as part of the exercises from the previous chapter.

- Frustration—People who are otherwise smart are not doing good work.
- Disappointment—Promising projects fail because of staff or student conflict.
- Worry—Your school lacks character or its climate does not feel safe or inclusive.
- Puzzlement—No unifying feeling makes a team out of the various individuals in your school.
- Sadness—Student or staff morale is low.
- Elation—Shared commitment exists to improve the sense of community in the school.
- Anger Disagreements about values and directions within the school or school system have surfaced and are pulling it apart.

Look for Negatives

The feelings you identified in the previous chapter form a jumping-off point for assessing your current situation. That situation is the product of the balance between positive and negative feelings. Addressing continuing sources of unpleasant feelings in your school is important because these sources can erode morale, trust, confidence, and focus. It is no less vital, however, to identify and build on strengths in your school. Ultimately, successful change borrows energy from positive areas.

First, though, continue the process to identify likely sources of negative feelings in your school. From the following list, consider which of these or similar situations seem to describe your school's problems:

- Staff members lack a coherent sense of direction.
- No feeling of community exists.
- Many different ideas about change vie for priority.
- Too many students and staff members don't feel like they belong.
- A spark of enthusiasm is lacking, though problems are minimal.
- Good ideas don't seem to get much support.
- Inertia has set in while the ship slowly sinks.
- Students' test scores are not as high as they could be.
- New approaches have no strong or lasting impact.
- Student-student, staff-staff, or staff-student conflict is too frequent.
- Isolated cliques or subgroups dominate the school culture.
- Decisions are made with great emotion; people cling to rejected ideas and take it personally when their views are not adopted.
- Staff or students often claim ignorance of the rules.
- Fixing blame is a common or first response to conflict.
- Staff or students strongly resist any change.

In each of these areas, social-emotional learning and character education initiatives are appropriate responses. The reasons for these types of programs may vary from area to area, but their common denominator is the importance of realigning relationships within your school. Social-emotional programs can become a force for positive change in schools, especially when they are brought in or broadened in ways that exemplify the programs' principles and a problem-solving approach.

In a problem-solving approach to implementing social-emotional learning and character education, you highlight, use, and expand on strengths even as you address shortcomings. Your understanding of the depth, strength, or intractability of your school's problems is clearest when you simultaneously look at your school's assets. Identifying existing sources of strength in your setting, the focus of the following sections, is a good way to initiate strong social-emotional efforts.

Strengths Underlying Social and Academic Success

The fields of organizational psychology, human performance, and brain-based learning have produced new perspectives on understanding strengths. Your ability to improve social-emotional learning and character education in your school can grow from insights gleaned from these areas.

Think of your school as being similar to a corporation. A corporation consists of groups of people legally constituted to act as if they were one person. And you know from experience that schools, like people, have their own personalities. A positive, constructive personality tends to arise when staff and students spend significant amounts of time engaged in activities reflecting their strengths. In social-emotional terms, these are times when staff and students are working in optimal performance states. You can see this when people carry out tasks with enthusiasm; if you ask them, they are likely to tell you that at those moments, they are using their various skills in challenging but attainable ways. You can better understand these moments and the strengths involved through the theory of multiple intelligences.

Multiple intelligences theory is familiar to most teachers as a set of instructional principles or aids, but its uses and significance are much deeper. You can glean this depth by looking at the concept from a historical and social-emotional perspective. In 1983, Howard Gardner proposed seven varieties of intelligences humans possess: linguistic, logical-mathematical, spatial, musical, bodily kinesthetic, interpersonal, and intrapersonal. Most recently, as his research has continued, Gardner has posited a naturalist and even a spiritual intelligence (National Professional Resources, 1998).

From a social-emotional point of view, these intelligences reflect ways in which individuals learn most effectively and deeply. They are best thought of as pathways through which learners' emotions can be engaged, their passions stirred, and learning transmitted not only to the mind but also to the heart. The way in which these pathways operate is outlined by the social-emotional learning principles mentioned earlier; through caring relationships, learning that is goal-directed, focused, purposeful, and linked with positive emotion is most likely to endure and translate into constructive action.

Learners (who include staff as well as students) are best reached through at least one of their multiple intelligences. Daniel Goleman's insight was to recognize that, while everyone may not be able to learn through linguistic, mathematical, spatial, musical, or any other particular intelligence, there seem to be no restrictions on anyone learning through interpersonal and intrapersonal intelligences (1995). The latter two, which Gardner referred to as personal intelligences, serve as the springboard for what Goleman called *emotional intelligence*.

Each person involved in a school—staff, students, parents, and administrators—has a different level of each type of intelligence. Similarly, the collective entity known as a school has its profile. Look at your school (or schools) and think about the individuals who comprise your school community. What is your school's profile of intelligences? Does that pattern, with its highs and lows, give you any insights into why you have the problems you do? As you clarify your understanding of the strengths and difficulties in your school, keep in mind that emotional intelligence—referred to in this book as social-emotional learning and character education—is the most broadly teachable of the multiple intelligences and the area through which you can most easily access less-developed intelligences.

Without social-emotional skills, a school cannot function as a caring community of sound character in which learning is productively put to use in the lives of students and in the fabric of their families and communities. Therefore, to solve problems in the functioning of your school or to enhance what is taking place, you must build on and develop social-emotional learning and character education in your students, as well as in parents and your staff.

Uncovering Strengths

In every school, there are staff members and students who typify the kind of behaviors that define social-emotional programs. These are people others turn to when faced with challenges; they solve problems without hurting others and they serve as models of what Maslow called fully functioning persons (1982). They are beacons of character in your school. How can you find out where personal and emotional intelligences are already put to good use in your school? Here are a few telltale signs, based on *Promoting Social and Emotional Learning: Guidelines for Educators* (Elias et al., 1997):

- *Teachers who*
  – Are socially popular, who people turn to for help, are liked and respected by all, are good problem solvers, etc.
  – Demonstrate caring for children.
  – Run groups effectively.
  – Take on tasks without concern for work hours and time involved.
  – Reach out strongly to parents.
- *Support staff members* who demonstrate concern for students, education, and the goals of the school.
- *Students* who have friends in different subgroups, accept leadership roles, or think about the school as a whole.

- *Parents* who present you with problems to solve rather than complaints, and care about issues other than those that affect their own children.

Identifying strengths is an important but all-too-often overlooked early step in creating positive change. Realism is essential. Who can be counted on? What do they have to contribute? Social-emotional learning and character education must be built on the existing foundation in your school. Rather than focus primarily on the weak points, it is ultimately more structurally sound (and emotionally intelligent) to work visibly from your school's strong points.

▼　　▼　　▼

Transitions: Review and a Look Ahead

Review

- Problem identification involves putting the issues that underlie your negative feelings into words, while avoiding placing blame.
- A better understanding of the strengths of your organization will point to supports for the change process and will bring problem statements into clearer focus.
- Sources of social-emotional strength can be found among teachers, support staff, parents, and students.
- Multiple intelligences theory, when applied to your school as a whole, can give you insight into the patterns of strengths and weaknesses you find.

Bridge

Having clarified feelings and looked at problems in terms of both shortcomings and strengths, you can now begin setting powerful and realistic goals. As you prepare for this process, consider your own overall goal. Perhaps you can capture this by creating a vision of what a caring community of learners in your school would look like. What would you list as components of such a dynamic community? To what extent do you want to build a community of learners, dedicated to promoting knowledgeable, responsible, non-violent, caring children and educators? What holds you back? What may keep your staff from joining you? What would motivate you and them? Chapter 5 shows how you can use goal setting to focus your change efforts and take a significant step toward action.

Reflections for Action

• Using your feelings as a barometer, how would you put social-emotional and character-related problems into words?

• What profiles of multiple intelligences—strengths and weak-nesses—do you see in your school?

• What areas of social-emotional strength or character quali-ties exist among your staff? Students? Parents? In your community?

• Where are social-emotional learning and character educa-tion being enhanced effectively in your classrooms? In your overall practices? In school or district goals? In what areas do these need to be strengthened?

• What steps can you take to check your perception of the problems and strengths in your school? Who could you enlist as allies?

Set Goals:
Focus the Change Efforts

Once you put problems into words, you can begin to set goals. Well-formulated goals are realistic, attainable, under control, and preeminently important. If you consider feelings catalysts for action, then consider goals the driving forces and guardrails as action moves ahead.

When you identify and clarify goals, you and your school are better able to concentrate your energy, resources, and action to achieve desired outcomes. This process becomes less and less simple as you uncover more and more concerns within your school. When you face multiple goals, you will need ways to prioritize them to focus efforts and make tangible progress in at least one area, followed by progress in other areas. Prioritizing, in turn, requires you to create an inclusive process where many voices have input into set directions. Although you may be tempted to short circuit this process in the name of efficiency, you will find that the more stakeholders have a say, the more satisfying, encompassing, and obtainable your goals become.

Some of the problems you identify may be immediate and intense; others may be large, complex, and long-standing. Bringing social-emotional learning and character education into schools is not designed to alleviate short-term problems. There is no quick fix to build character or create a caring community of learners, but your emphasis on social and character issues will bolster an element of your school that is essential for success in this era of high academic standards. Begin by establishing a few specific, highly focused, and attainable goals. As you bring in your new program to address these social-emotional goals, you simultaneously build your capacity to make progress in meeting other, related goals.

Seek a Social-Emotional Program Mentor

At this point, begin a process that will be extremely important throughout your efforts to bring social-emotional programs into your school: seek a mentor. When your students learn something new, you certainly expect them to seek the advice of those with more experience, typically an adult or older peer. When your teachers are exposed to a new curriculum, you no doubt do your best to provide them with support and encouragement. As an administrator, you are no more capable of going through change in isolation. Doing so would neglect the valuable contributions a mentoring relationship can provide. Any time you develop a new skill, the path you travel contains emotional ups and downs. You experience frustration over difficulties that must be overcome and pride about successes that you will want to share. Those who have sucessfully gone down the path before can offer tremendous practical advice and emotional support.

Who can fill this mentoring role? Here are a few possibilities, but these should in no way limit your thinking:

- A member of the Collaborative for Academic, Social, and Emotional Learning (CASEL) Administrators Network (http://www.casel.org) or a member of the HOPE Foundation's School Leadership Network (http://www.communitiesofhope.org).
- A colleague in a school that has implemented a social-emotional or character education program or someone from a school or district that has received a National Schools of Character Award (information can be found at http://www.casel.org and http://www.character.org).
- A consultant from a similar program.
- An administrator, master teacher, or other educator familiar with the process of organizational change.

Prioritize and Set Goals for Your School

You may have experienced what often happens as a result of identifying problems: You accumulate a dizzying and sometimes contradictory array of areas that need to be addressed. Certainly, circumstances exist when one or two clearly defined areas of concern emerge, but this tends to be the exception. As noted earlier, you will find it essential to prioritize. Three interrelated steps are useful in setting these priorities:

1. Group problems into larger, more encompassing areas that allow more people and resources to come together and create potential for synergistic problem solving.

2. Review your list with your mentor or a social-emotional learning resource person and discuss the order in which it makes sense to tackle various areas.

3. Solicit the opinions of various constituencies and stakeholders involved in defining the problems.

Grouping problems is very helpful and can occur in several ways. You, your mentor, or the stakeholders can sit with a list of problem areas and attempt to create groupings that make sense. With a narrowed list in front of you, you will find that discussion priorities are a bit easier to manage. Work done by CASEL and Character Education Partnership (CEP) also can assist in grouping and goal setting. Both organizations looked at many case examples where schools have succeeded—and failed—in effectively implementing such innovations and improving school character and climate (Elias et al., 1997; Farmer, 1999). As part of this review, CASEL and CEP focused on the kinds of goals that were set, and then identified five primary areas that serve as fruitful entry points for bringing social-emotional programs into a school or district (originally presented in Chapter 1):

1. Establish a school climate articulating specific themes, character elements, or values.

2. Increase explicit instruction in social-emotional and character skills.

3. Increase explicit instruction in health-promotion and problem-prevention skills.

4. Set up systems to enhance coping skills and social support for transitions, crises, and resolving conflicts.

5. Create widespread, systematic opportunities for positive, contributory service.

At this stage, your level of background knowledge will be critical. If you have little or no background, your goal may simply be to learn more about the concepts and processes from books or visits to sites where those programs operate (key resources are listed in Appendix D). If your school has passed the beginning stages, the work of CASEL and CEP provides some guideposts to help set new goals in conjunction with the considerations already mentioned.

Here are some possible goals for schools looking for the next step in developing or expanding their programs (see Chapter 10 for elaboration of these and related ideas):

• Set up a social-emotional learning and character education administrative/curricular structure or committee to advance the progress of the programs throughout the school.
• Improve monitoring methods.
• Increase staff responsibility for professional development around social-emotional learning and character education, especially for those new to their roles.
• Cultivate greater staff leadership and commitment to these programs.
• Move toward making your school a learning organization that works with emotional intelligence.

▼   ▼   ▼

Transitions: Review and a Look Ahead

Review

• While formulating goals, make sure your goals are realistic, highly specific, focused, attainable, under your control, and of preeminent importance.
• By obtaining stakeholders' input in prioritizing your goals, you involve them in the process in a meaningful way.
• Base your goals on your level of background knowledge; different starting points call for different goals.
• A mentor can be a valuable resource as you proceed through the change process.

Bridge

Before you move to the next step of the process, which focuses on finding alternative ways to get to your goals, take a moment to do one final goal-setting activity. Exploring your feelings and those of your staff has been a part of the process to this point. There are times, however, when our deepest feelings can be elusive. To ensure that important goals are not still hidden, ask yourself the first three questions that appear in the "Reflections for Action" section of this chapter.

The answers may provide you with additional goals—or important perspectives on goals already identified—as you move toward seeking solutions. These questions ask you to confront realistically your willingness to change things that, at some level, you have known for a while are not productive. Unless you are aware of these areas of hesitation, they can exercise hidden influences on you as you lead your staff and school through the change process. Having a mentor provides an important sense of perspective and a sounding board as you move into generating ways to reach your goals.

Reflections for Action

- If you have the necessary courage, what is one practice you are doing in your school that you would stop doing?
- If you have the necessary courage, what is one practice you are not doing in your school that you would start doing?
- If you have the necessary courage, what is something you are doing in your school that you question and would finally want to resolve?
- How have you used mentors—formally and informally—most successfully in the past? Knowing this, what roles could a social-emotional mentor play for you?

Generate Options:
Think of Many Things to Do

Brainstorming is a time-honored principle, and one that is well aligned with modern brain research. Individuals tend to prefer a nonjudgmental environment when they need to generate multiple ways to try to reach goals. Data also suggest that the best and most creative solutions emerge later in the brainstorming process, not at the beginning. In addition, brainstorming has the potential for involving many different people in the solution-finding process (Caine and Caine, 1997).

Promote Brainstorming

Your task as an educational leader is to create contexts in which different groups of individuals feel comfortable brainstorming lots of ways to reach goals you and they have set. Caine and Caine (1997) suggest that you can reduce threat and anxiety by helping staff members feel safe to try, think, speculate, create, and make mistakes on their way to excellence.

Think of one creative thing you have done. What conditions allowed you to do it? What are some different ways you can create the conditions that will encourage the creativity of others you work with regarding social-emotional learning and character education? Identify the kind of environment in which you feel most comfortable brainstorming and encourage others to do the same. The following are some effective approaches to fostering creativity and "out of the box" thinking:

- Move meetings off site.
- Make meetings less formal.
- Take breaks for moments of reflection.
- Allow time for personal sharing of successes in related situations.
- Use a variety of formats and opportunities for paired, small group, and large group interaction.
- Encourage multiple modalities for expression, including art and music.

It is essential to generate many options before deciding on a course of action. Your goals for change will be best served, however, if you also examine what other schools have attempted or accomplished. The experience of administrators who have successfully brought social-emotional programs into their schools will help on many levels. Try to focus on what has been tried by other schools whose characteristics and problems are similar to yours. Consult with your mentor. Look in the literature and at key Web sites for other programs that address your concerns (see Appendix D for suggested resources). Of course, keep your intuitive antennae poised to pick up which examples are potential solutions for your situation and which ones are popular just because of their marketing strategies. In the words of Wheatley and Kellner-Rogers (1996, p. 21):

> Observing others' successes can show us new possibilities, expand our thinking, trigger our creativity. But their experience can never provide models that will work the same for us. It is good to be inquisitive; it is hopeless to believe that they have discovered our answers.

At this point, do not get bogged down in logistics. Brainstorm. Be creative. Each of your possible choices will be examined before detailed planning begins. In fact, to broaden the richness of options being considered, delegate some of this exploration to teachers and other staff in your school. In addition to the help it can provide in widening the search, delegation is an interesting first step to get others involved. As you and your team explore options, you may want to organize several sharing and brainstorming opportunities to take advantage of the increasing amount and breadth of information you and others obtain.

Here are some other ways to help you and your staff get more enthused about the possibilities for social-emotional or character education in your school:

- Consider changing some cultural factors that will lay the groundwork for new programs, such as how and when meetings are scheduled, or what expectations are for communication with parents and students.
- Set up study committees or task forces to look into specific areas and report back with a list of ideas at a designated time and place.

- Determine how to introduce staff members to what new programs involve and resemble (for example, schedule an "awareness" presentation from a trainer or a visit to a school implementing such a program).
- Introduce a pilot program. Think about where this could be possible. For example, would the health program be a place to start? Would teachers at a certain grade level be particularly motivated?
- Contact other schools to gather ideas about practices they used to begin or expand their own initiatives.

How to Organize and Shape Your Information and Options

You can organize your search and brainstorming by referring to the five domains presented in Chapter 1, or by starting with whatever other categories you have used to group ideas and make goal statements. Most solutions and ideas fit best under one of these domains, although sometimes one or more new domains emerge. Building your personal social, emotional, and character skills can also fit within this framework, as can building the skills of students, staff, and parents.

All the ideas you generate have to move beyond the "idea" stage. They have to be translated into some kind of "delivery system." Regardless of the specific goal areas you are working with, they can be organized in several ways. The following are some possibilities.

Establish a school climate articulating specific themes, character elements, and values. Set up themes for each grade level in a high school and have readings, assemblies, and various projects linked to them. Use advisory periods in middle and junior high schools to discuss social-emotional issues, analyze values in media, and conduct problem-solving and conflict resolution sessions around student concerns. At the elementary level, hold morning meetings to help students transition into the school day. At the beginning of the school year, plan discussions in each class that give students answers to these questions:

- In this class, what should I do when I don't understand what is being taught?
- In this class, what should I do when I am very angry?
- In this class, what should I do when I am upset by things happening outside of class and can't concentrate on my work?
- In this class, what should I do when I want to let people know they did a good job or were helpful to me?
- In this class, what are respectful ways to disagree with one another?

See the Character Education Partnership Web site (http://www.character.org) for examples of promising practices and examples from schools that have won the National Schools of Character award.

Increase explicit instruction in social-emotional learning life skills and social competencies. Bring in a well-validated curriculum to serve as the hub of your efforts. Examples at the elementary level include Second Step, PATHS, Open Circle, The Responsive Classroom, I Can Problem Solve, and Social Decision Making/Social Problem Solving. At the secondary level, options include the Resolving Conflict Creatively Program, Quest International's Skills for Adolescence and Skills for Action programs, the Giraffe program, and Facing History and Ourselves (see http://www.casel.org for further information and additional examples).

Increase explicit instruction in health-promotion and problem-prevention skills. Programs such as Growing Healthy, Life Skills Training, and Olweus's work in bully prevention provide developmentally sensitive, explicit

instruction in skills for health promotion and in targeted prevention of smoking, substance use, and violence.
Information regarding programs of this type can be obtained
through the American School Health Association at
www.ashaweb.org and the U.S. Department of Education at
www.ed.gov/offices/OESE/SDFS/programs.html.

**Set up systems to enhance coping skills and social
support for transitions, crises, and resolving conflicts.**
Set up groups for students whose families are experiencing
significant stress, such as serious medical difficulty, bereave-
ment, separation and divorce, and unemployment. Provide
programs for parents to manage their stress and to build their
social-emotional skills in relation to parenting (see the
Emotionally Parenting Web Site at http://www.EQParenting
.com for more information). Institute a grade-level or school-
wide conflict resolution program modeled on the Resolving
Conflict Creatively Program or the Colorado School
Mediation Project, both of which are based on all students
having a basic understanding of conflict resolution and build
their specific peer mediation and conflict resolution
processes on top of that understanding.

**Create widespread, systematic opportunities for
positive, contributory service.** Preschoolers and elementary school children can each be assigned some role in the
classroom that reflects their contribution to it; you can extend
their concern to the hallways around the classroom and to
the school buildings as they get older. Secondary school students can provide service by contributing to the environment
outside and around the school and in the community. The
Giraffe program and Quest International's Skills for Action
provide exemplary guidelines for maximizing students' benefits from service opportunities.

▼　▼　▼

Transitions: Review and a Look Ahead

Review

• Generating options involves brainstorming and exploring ideas from as many sources as possible. Do not be concerned with your opinions regarding the strength and feasibility of these ideas at this stage.

• You must create comfortable, safe environments for brainstorming to flourish.

• The brainstorming process benefits from involving many brains in the "storming." Delegate some of the responsibility for generating options to teachers, staff, and parents.

• The options generated should have an action or service delivery component, perhaps tied into the five social-emotional domains.

Bridge

This chapter emphasized ways you can maximize possibilities and participation for creative brainstorming in your school. The quality of your ultimate solution will relate to the quantity and diversity of options you consider and the seriousness of commitment of those who generate the options. In the next chapter, each of these options must be carefully examined. This process will be helped by the extent to which you create a climate where participants are more interested in improving social-emotional or character education programs in your school than in seeing their particular ideas enacted. There is no way to guarantee this will occur. However, the process you have followed so far and the steps for considering consequences outlined in Chapter 7 are based on procedures designed to address latent opposition and counterproductive forces. Examining potential outcomes is as much an art as a science.

Reflections for Action

- To what degree do you believe brainstorming can be advantageous even though it slows down the process? What feelings do you have about opening up the process to new ideas and input?
- Which teachers, staff, or parents can you think of who could help generate programming options?
- Under which social-emotional domain(s) do most of your options fall? What might this tell you about the functioning of your school?
- Where do you see your staff freely and openly exchanging ideas? Based on this, what is one step you can take to foster an environment conducive to brainstorming?

▲　▲　▲

Envision Outcomes:
Consider All the Consequences

Organizations cannot sustain an infinite number of change initiatives. Therefore, you must pay careful attention to all promising solutions to explore their ramifications. Before deciding on a course of action, you must evaluate the likely consequences of each of your proposed solutions. The envisioning process is an excellent way to achieve this in a realistic, practical manner.

Of course, the best envisioning occurs in hindsight, and this chapter represents the hindsight derived from several program implementations. Sometimes, resources are not as plentiful as they appear to be; impending staff changes can create unforeseen negative consequences, and the school can be less ready for some options than for others. Entrenched factions lobbying for different ways to proceed might make some roads far more difficult to travel than they had first appeared. Realities can't be ignored. But potentially negative consequences do not have to bring needed efforts to a dead stop. Usually, you must consider a balance of positives and negatives—short and long term—for various constituencies and then devise a systematic way to evaluate the outcome of these possibilities. At the least, school members who help anticipate what might happen if they approach social-emotional learning and character education in a certain way tend to be more forgiving if things do not work out well. They know a serious effort was made to look ahead.

Having picked several areas in which to focus your efforts, it is time to consider the consequences, or outcomes, of the changes and innovations you are considering. This step will help you refine your problem statement or goal by identifying criteria for measuring progress.

As you think about outcomes, remember that actions may have both positive and negative ramifications that can reverberate beyond the actions' immediate focus. Bronfenbrenner's ecological theory provides a useful framework for thinking through the possibilities (Bronfenbrenner, 1979). He suggests considering the following areas when looking at the impact of a course of action:

• How will it affect the individuals who have to make the changes? How well are they prepared, in terms of prior history, temperament, skills, and specific training?
• How will it affect the small-group contexts in which people work together intensively and regularly and therefore exercise interdependent influence on one another? Examples of what Bronfenbrenner calls "microsystems" include
  – classrooms
  – grade-level faculty
  – subject-area faculty
  – members of "houses" or similar units within schools

- various classes that students take (including art, physical education, or music)
- informal times such as lunch, recess, dismissal, and class changes
- faculty meetings
- other faculty and home-school groups
- union representatives
- special-services staff, guidance, and other pupil-services providers
- support staff
- business units
- administrative teams

Be sure to consider how any option will affect the nature of the interactions within each of these contexts because this will influence the outcome of your new initiative.

- How will it affect the culture and climate of the school as a unit?
- How will it affect relationships with parents, groups and constituencies in the community, state-level education authorities, and other relevant state, regional, and federal bodies?

No doubt, you have found that a change in procedures surrounding discipline, for example, affects students most directly, but also has consequences for staff development, parental concerns, resources, political considerations, and logistics. Bringing in a social-emotional or character curriculum has consequences related to the following:

- Staff experiences with previous curricula.
- Other curricula that may be used in grade levels prior to and after those in which the new program is planned.
- Instructional technologies and how they fit with existing pedagogy and resources.

- The match with what other schools in the district might be doing.
- Relevance to local, state, or national "standards."
- The nature of training and ongoing coaching and supervision and its cost in terms of time, money, and other resources.

Envisioning outcomes always requires strong consideration of the time and resources needed to reach a state of readiness in any area. Your mentor, CASEL, and the CEP can be invaluable sources of advice because they can share specific experiences and help you think through possibilities.

How and Why to Envision

The use of the word "envision" reflects advances in emotional intelligence theory and hearkens back to the first step in the problem-solving process: focusing on signs of feelings. Looking at outcomes cannot be dispassionate. Here are some key questions for which you will want to solicit genuine answers:

- How will it feel to carry out a particular option, in the short, medium, and long term?
- What can be done to make the experience more positive, better supported, more likely to succeed and favorably viewed?
- How will it feel if you and your school decide *not* to carry out a particular option in the short, medium, and long term?
- How will you know when and how your efforts are succeeding? What will positive outcomes look like? At all the relevant levels, what indicators will tell how your initiative is doing, how it is affecting the school, and what changes should be made to improve goal attainment?

The subjective calculus for answering these questions requires working in a spirit of improvement, not optimization. Sometimes, problems demand the best action you and your school can take in a given time frame. You do not have the luxury of postponing action until you can explore every option. On the other hand, in certain situations, there is more time available and decision making can proceed in that light. Usually, though, you will be comparing potential courses of action to the status quo in addition to reviewing them on their own merits. As noted earlier, any solution and plan is subject to the action-research process (see Appendix C), which involves ongoing monitoring and adjustments.

Schwahn and Spady (1998) point out that lasting change requires strong, positive mobilization. Therefore, you should ensure that envisioning beneficial outcomes, however small, plays a prominent part in the process you use to consider consequences.

Your task as an administrator is to take the options from the previous chapter and set up a structure that ensures each one is given specific consideration. One way to do this is to use the "options and outcomes" procedure. Actually, this is a fancy title for a variation of the old process of diagramming sentences. For each option you generate, draw lines to allow the listing of possible consequences if it is followed. Some of these lines are labeled so that specific aspects of consequences are reviewed, such as short- and long-term effects; implications for staff, students, and parents; and other considerations mentioned in this chapter, suggested by your mentor, or generated in the course of problem solving and planning in your school.

Figure 7.1 contains a sample of the options and outcomes procedure for one option ("Option A") to a hypothetical decision. In this example, the decision makers are interested in three areas: long-term outcomes, short-term outcomes, and implications for staff. You would write possible consequences

Figure 7.1
Options and Outcomes

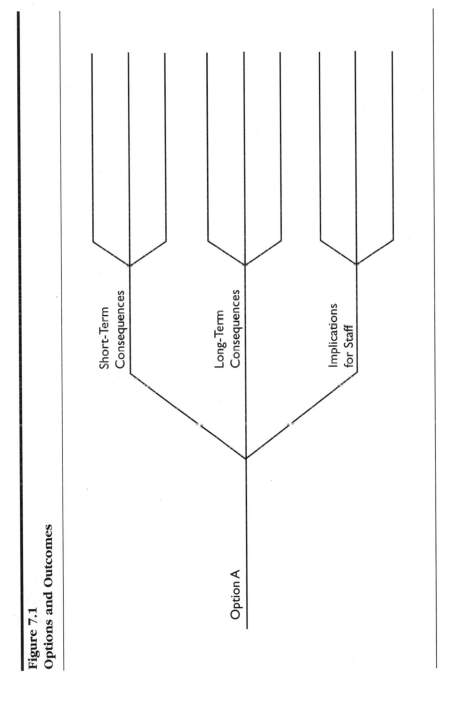

for each of these areas in the branches of the chart. The procedure would be repeated for each possible option.

There are many ways to organize this process to maximize staff involvement, including:

- Assigning staff subgroups to envision outcomes for one or more options.
- Conducting the review process as a committee of the whole.
- Asking different constituent groups to envision outcomes from their unique perspectives.
- Convening interdisciplinary groups to generate outcomes that will incorporate a shared perspective.
- Employing a staging process in which a subgroup conducts an initial screening of a large number of options.

Regardless of the method you choose, you will find it useful to create checklists to help groups organize their work and carry out the diagramming process. How much detail you provide to guide the process is a strategic decision. For example, in some cases, you may wish to provide more general instructions if your intent is to foster greater group creativity in envisioning outcomes.

▼ ▼ ▼

Transitions: Review and a Look Ahead

Review

- Envisioning the range of consequences—negative and positive, long and short term—associated with your options helps determine which option holds the greatest potential to help you reach your goal.

- Bronfenbrenner's ecological theory suggests interventions in one aspect of programming may have far-reaching ramifications. As you envision outcomes, think of possible outcomes that extend beyond the target of the intervention.

- Though a "perfect" solution is unlikely, solutions should be compared in terms of how it would feel to enact the solution, how it would feel not to, and what may change in the school as a result.

- The options and outcomes procedure, a method of diagramming options and consequences, can be helpful in organizing your envisioning results.

Bridge

By this time, you have set a goal for improving the social and emotional climate and character of your school and have arrived at specific options for achieving this goal. The step emphasized in this chapter, anticipating outcomes for various options, amounts to predicting the future. You need only ask your local weatherman or stockbroker to learn how easy that is. As you anticipate outcomes, stay in close communication with your mentor and review information about how other schools similar to yours set up programs. Their experience with implementing similar options can be instructive in your efforts to predict outcomes in your school.

Your ability to bring various options together in a creative and viable approach is important. No less important, however, is your ability to articulate a vision for the changes you hope to achieve and to keep this vision salient in the eyes of your staff. What's the big picture? Why are you doing all this? These and other questions will call on you to be clear about the specific outcomes you want to achieve. The process of bringing social-emotional initiatives into a school or district is dynamic. Discussing outcomes in a serious way serves to sharpen the vision of where the organization needs to be and can be. It becomes a matter of clarifying your vision and recognizing that, as with any visioning process, lenses do need to be cleaned off and adjusted at times.

The next chapter describes the process of moving toward a particular approach that will become the basis of action planning. Just how smooth that process will be depends on how much you and your staff share a vision and agree that you have fairly considered a range of options.

Reflections for Action

• Observe your feelings and those of your staff as you envision outcomes:

— Which outcomes seem to generate excitement and enthusiasm?

— Which outcomes are associated with feelings of frustration or anger?

— Why are these options generating these emotions?

• Using Bronfenbrenner's ecological theory as a guide, who will be affected by bringing social-emotional and character education programs to your school, and how might people react? Think in terms of individuals, small-group microsystems, the school as a whole, and the broader community.

• What new relationships may be created, or which old relationships changed, by bringing such programs to your school?

▲ ▲ ▲

Choose Carefully:
Select a Goal-Oriented or Goal-Driven Solution

When organizations engage in a thorough decision-making process, they typically uncover several pathways that seem possible to follow. Rarely, if ever, is one perfect. When the focus of decision making relates to matters as complex and interpersonally based as social-emotional learning and character education, the choices are often more numerous and less clear.

At this point, you need to keep one question foremost in your mind: What will help you reach *your* goals and what is *your* best solution (i.e., the one most workable in your particular situation and context)? Focusing on your goals keeps you and your school from becoming distracted. Otherwise, you are likely to encounter dilution of efforts, lack of clarity, or compromises that will be politically satisfying but won't produce effective programs for your students.

A Decision Matrix Framework for Making Goal-Driven Choices

How will you choose among the options you identified? Almost certainly, the "options and outcomes" procedure from Chapter 7 will raise potential negative consequences for each option. Because there is no "perfect" solution, you and your staff will benefit enormously from using a framework to sort out the options you have developed. The framework in this chapter can help you make the necessary choices and avoid decision-making paralysis.

The decision-making process is a combination of objective and subjective data. You have worked to gather input from diverse sources; each will want to know that their ideas and concerns were taken seriously. Therefore, you and your staff will find it useful to have some structure for introducing objectivity into the decision-making process. There is no problem with introducing the subjective opinions; these, without doubt, will find their way into the process. A decision matrix is one model for systematically reviewing options and weighing outcomes. It includes steps that help group members become conscious of what goes into a decision, and provides a structure that helps the group look at the issues in a relatively objective manner.

A Caveat Before Beginning

Before you begin, you should make one final examination of whether you have incorporated all the input necessary for sound organizational decision making. Before deriving action based on the decision matrix, determine the following:

- The extent to which you have meaningfully involved various constituents.
- Whether you and your staff heard all points of view, including those in the minority.
- Whether you have faced conflict and have made genuine attempts to resolve differences.
- How well you have communicated that any point of view may turn out to be correct or may contribute elements to the final plan.
- What process you have set up to revisit the decision in a reasonable amount of time.

After reviewing these considerations and gathering any additional input needed, you can initiate the completion of the decision matrix as a way of moving toward focused action.

Instructions for Completing the Decision Matrix

The decision matrix, like virtually all problem-solving approaches, helps people choose between alternatives somewhat objectively. When there is more than one decision to make, you will find it wise to complete a separate matrix for each one. For example, bringing social-emotional learning and character education curricula into an elementary school and a middle school are separate decisions. After making each decision, you will need to ensure their compatibility and create the necessary continuities between them. Other decisions might involve the nature of staff development and parent education for social-emotional or character program efforts. These decisions, though ultimately in need of coordination, should first be made based on their own specific goals and circumstances.

No procedure is perfect; consider the decision matrix as a suggestion that has proven helpful in many situations.

Following are instructions for its use. Consider laying out this format on a series of newsprints or on a large, white marker board. A sample matrix form is included in Figure 8.1 to help you visualize the procedure more easily. Figure 8.2 contains a sample of a completed matrix to determine whether to institute a "morning meeting" in the classroom.

The most important criterion for the decision makers in Figure 8.2 is that the option chosen must have a significant effect on the school. They are also interested in minimizing the class time used and keeping costs and training time low. Option B1, "No meetings at all," keeps class time, costs, and training low, but has no desired effect on students. In this instance, option A1 would be chosen. The score indicates its strength in the most important criterion (effect) while being minimally lower on other criteria than option C1. To use the matrix, follow these 10 steps:

1. Describe the decision to be made.

2. At the top of the columns labeled A1, B1, C1, etc. under "options," describe in a few key words each of the alternatives you are considering. Refer back to the work you did in the previous chapters as well as the final considerations raised in the preceding section of this chapter.

3. In the column headed "criteria," describe the dimensions of the problem that you feel are important and must be considered as you examine each alternative (e.g., cost, time, effect on staff, effect on students). Principles of backward planning apply here; it helps to visualize the way things will look when everything is in place and desired outcomes are being met (Wiggins & McTighe, 1998).

4. Identify the criterion that is *least important* to you and in the "priority" column number it "1"; the next most important criterion, number "2." Continue rating the criteria in order of their importance with the most important one receiving the highest number.

Figure 8.1
Decision Matrix

Decision: _____
_____
_____

Criteria	Priority	Options					
		A1	A2	B1	B2	C1	C2
		TOTAL:		TOTAL:		TOTAL:	

Figure 8.2
Sample Decision Matrix

Decision: *Should we hold "morning meetings" in our classes as a way of greeting students and introducing SEL/CE?*

Criteria	Priority	Options					
		A1 Yes— meetings in all classes	A2	B1 No meetings at all	B2	C1 Start in one grade	C2
Costs kept low	3	4	12	5	15	4	12
Uses little class time	1	2	2	5	5	3	3
Low training needs	2	2	4	5	10	4	8
High impact on school	4	5	20	0	0	3	12
		TOTAL:	38	**TOTAL:**	30	**TOTAL:**	35

5 = highly likely; 4 = likely; 3 = somewhat likely; 2 = slightly likely; 1 = not likely

5. Examine the first option in light of the first criterion. Estimate the degree to which that alternative meets that criterion. Rate this degree on a scale of 1 to 5, with 5 indicating that the option will be highly likely to meet the criterion. Place the appropriate number in the box in column A1 alongside the first criterion.

6. Examine the same option in light of the next criterion and insert the value you are placing on it in column A1.

7. Continue the process with all criteria for each option. (You may vary the procedure by going across each option for one criterion at a time.)

8. Multiply the priority rating of the criteria with the likelihood rating in columns A1, B1, C1, etc., and put the result in columns A2, B2, C2, etc.

9. Total the results under columns A2, B2, C2, etc.

10. The column with the highest total represents the alternative that best meets all of your criteria. It is possible that more than one alternative will receive a high score. In that case, you might consider a combination of alternatives as a new solution to your problem.

Ground Rules for Decision Making

Remember, completing the decision matrix is usually an interpersonal process. It is a way to minimize the subjectivity in decision making, but it does not eliminate it. You are most likely to use the matrix when you would like to have two or more people cooperate in arriving at a decision. It is unrealistic to believe everyone will always be happy with the process used and willing to compromise gladly when their favorite solutions are not completely accepted. With that in mind, here are some ground rules that add to the quality of the process and the integrity of the information in decision making and increase the likelihood of winning supporters as the action plan moves forward:

- Ensure everyone has the right to speak openly, with trust, and without interruption.

- Elicit differing views to both broaden considerations and reinforce expectations that diverse ideas are honestly treasured.

- Focus on best-case outcomes and use backward planning in creative ways to encourage sharing of visions of how success will look.

- Use a variety of techniques to arrive at consensus, such as posting options and giving participants three to five votes each to distribute as they wish; asking proponents of options to argue against themselves and for other options; and working in teams to combine existing options into new ones.

There are also specific techniques for generating new alternatives or clarifying and prioritizing criteria. For numerous suggestions in this area, see the sections on systems thinking and wheels of learning in *Schools That Learn: A Fifth Discipline Fieldbook*, by Peter Senge and colleagues (Doubleday, 2000). Senge's techniques include "Casual Loop Models," which help clarify connections and priorities, and the "Iceburg," where asking yourself a series of questions about school events, patterns, systemic structures, and your own thought patterns opens up new ways of acting.

▼ ▼ ▼

Transitions: Review and a Look Ahead

Review

- The decision matrix is a structured framework for choosing among options.

• Using the decision matrix involves comparing your criteria for accepting or rejecting an option with the extent to which each option achieves each criterion.

• Because all decisions involve subjectivity, group input will assist you in using the decision matrix.

• You will need to make sure that all involved in the decision-making process have a chance to voice opinions and concerns.

Bridge

Making a decision about a course of action signals the end of one informal stage of implementing social-emotional and character education programs and the start of another. You are moving from knowing what you want to make happen to making it happen. Paradoxically, the actions you will take next involve careful, detailed planning. The decision you have made is like the bare bones of passed legislation. You have to provide the details, and you cannot move confidently toward your selected program innovations until these details are elaborated. Chapter 9 guides you through the planning process.

Reflections for Action

• What steps can you take to ensure differing opinions about your decision get a chance to be heard?

• Which decision criteria are most important to you personally? Which are most important to your staff? If discrepancies between the two exist, how can these be reconciled?

• On which issues do you find it most difficult to compromise? Why?

• Of the potential outcomes of your decision, which are most exciting to you? Which do you consider to be areas of potential difficulty to look out for?

Plan Prescriptively:
Anticipate All Details and Roadblocks

Too often, good ideas end up being just that—ideas, rather than actualities. Getting good ideas to work involves more than is typically recognized. Even if you know what you would like to achieve, you need to be clear about how to get there. An analogy is a driver who has the street address for a destination, but no directions for reaching it. With this in mind, this chapter provides approaches to better plan how to achieve the options you selected for improving your school's initiatives for social-emotional learning and character education.

Detailed action requires you to articulate the specific steps involved in carrying out an idea. Your plan should anticipate pitfalls and roadblocks, as well as answer questions about who, what, where, why, and how. This planning process is likely to uncover adjustments you and other staff members must make to adapt your chosen initiatives to the specifics of your setting. In implementing these programs, you have an important opportunity to do more than initiate a specific plan. As you work through the action-planning process, your own actions can model social-emotional and character principles (see Chapter 1).

An Action-Planning Process

Creating a climate for social-emotional and character programs identifies resources, allies, rough spots, and resisters and serves as the start of a dynamic action-planning process. This process is outlined in Figure 9.1. Ultimately, two series of questions are required. As you take action, you must ask these questions continually and use the answers as part of the planning process.

The first series of questions relates to assigning tasks and considering the details that are required to implement your plan.

- What actions need to be taken to carry out the program initiative?
- What roles need to be filled?
- What are the skills needed to fill each role?
- Who are the candidates to fill them? Are they internal? If so, who will take their current roles?
- What structures need to be created? What changes in procedure need to be made? What resources, including time, need to be allocated to support the work of the roles and structures?
- What are potential roadblocks that these questions raise?

Figure 9.1
Action-Planning Flowchart

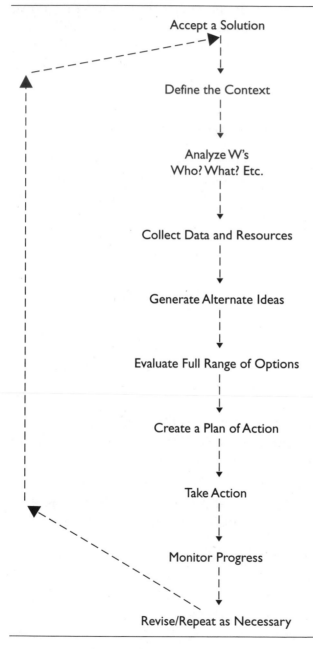

Accept a Solution

Define the Context

Analyze W's
Who? What? Etc.

Collect Data and Resources

Generate Alternate Ideas

Evaluate Full Range of Options

Create a Plan of Action

Take Action

Monitor Progress

Revise/Repeat as Necessary

The second series of questions relates to reflecting on the process as it unfolds. Reflective planning is designed to foster self-monitoring, self-awareness, and self-improvement. We encourage reflection by asking the people we work with to take another look at what they are doing, what they are planning, what they have done, and their reasons, reactions, and alternative methods. There are several aspects of reflective planning, represented by these questions:

- What did you like about what you did? What did not go the way you planned?
- What happened that you were not expecting?
- What would you do differently next time? What will you do next? What else might you do?
- How else can you do that/how else can that be done/how have others done this?
- What would it take for you to be confident of success?
- How did you decide to do what you did?
- What do you believe accounts for the outcomes that occurred?

The opportunity for you and the staff members on your planning team to answer these questions as part of the action-planning process allows you to tailor your initiatives to the context and available resources and to continually refine the implementation process.

What If Roadblocks Appear?

W. G. Tierney (2001) has found resistance to change can often be traced to five organizational factors as follows:

1. People do not agree on the problem to be solved or the goal to be pursued.
2. Time frames and working structures are not clear.
3. There is little accountability or monitoring and few benchmarks for implementation.

4. Changes are not communicated, or if they are, it is not done with perspective and care.

5. The system is frozen; people come to feel "why bother" and nothing happens or changes.

Here is how Tierney suggests you dislodge each of these roadblocks, in corresponding order:

1. Foster an atmosphere of agreement. Reopen discussions to a limited degree, but more broadly if necessary. Reconsider goals. Be sure that those who feel excluded have a say, especially opinion leaders, but mobilize positive opinion leaders to visibly engage in the discussions to illustrate the consensus already achieved.

2. Define roles and time frames. Specify who is going to do what, by when. Find out who cannot carry out all of their role(s) and make plans around that. Create a spirit in which bringing a good program into a school is more important than concealing that someone cannot do what is expected.

3. Seek comparative data. Look at how similar institutions do similar things. Seek advice from mentors and the network of practitioners. However, be sure to give yourself credit for your own progress.

4. Ensure good communication. Discuss how you will disseminate information, how much and by whom. Frequent communication is essential early in the implementation process. Set up ways for people to acknowledge that they have received your communiqués.

5. Encourage an innovation-friendly culture. Help people see change in a positive context, in the spirit of continuous improvement. Adaptation to changing realities is an ethical and professional responsibility. So is developing character in students and providing them—and staff—with safe, caring, challenging, and supportive learning environments to which they feel they can connect and contribute.

How to Build a Climate for a Genuine, Systemic Program

Regardless of the specific plans you are going to implement, much of your success will be influenced by the overall climate of your school. If you think about this in gardening terms, then the analogy is to preparing the soil for planting. While there are nuances of difference depending on the particular seeds you plan to grow, there are some basic principles of soil aeration, moisture, and care that will make it more likely that just about any healthy seed or seedling you plant will flourish. Similarly, as action planning proceeds in your school, there are some climate factors that will support whatever specific efforts you undertake in social-emotional learning or character education. You can determine the status of these factors in your school by asking yourself a series of questions:

- Who are the heroes and heroines you regularly point to in your talks and conversations? What kind of role models are they? Do they demonstrate the kind of behavior you want to encourage?
- What stories do you regularly tell about your school? Do they support the kind of behavior you want employees and students to emulate?
- How do you run meetings? Do people look forward to and willingly participate in your meetings?
- What ceremonies or school rituals, including assemblies, do you employ? What mix of aspects of your program do they represent? For example, do you open each day with words of encouragement or reflection, and do assemblies highlight service learning accomplishments? Are the majority of these rituals related to your priority values or do they emphasize minor or secondary goals?
- When people work together in groups in your school, do they do so in an efficient, effective way?

The following section outlines some suggestions for strengthening the emotional climate of your school.

Foster Identification with Local Heroes or Heroines

For examples, use people who demonstrate the kind of behavior you want to encourage. Brag about staff members, students, or parents who were calm in emergencies, or who solve problems by focusing on the problem, not on who was at fault or who can be blamed. Sometimes, the people with the best emotional intelligence are not the ones who hand in all their reports on time or score the most points in their sport or have the best political connections in town.

Engage in Active Storytelling

Tell stories conveying messages that strengthen your primary values or goals. Tell anecdotes that relate events in which people took reasonable risks and the results turned out well, and use examples that involve nonprofessional staff or community members. The process of thinking about appropriate stories will help you discover where good things are happening.

Furthermore, encourage staff to tell stories and to share stories with one another in electronic or print newsletters. This exchange can build better practice and foster mutual problem solving and support, and can be sent home to parents or included in community newsletters.

Send press releases to local newspapers that relate stories about staff and students. Parents and community residents are more interested than you might think in the projects your school undertakes in the social-emotional and character arena. One superintendent in Massachusetts created collages of all of the articles in local newspapers about his students' community service projects. He updated them constantly and displayed them prominently to parents, the school board, and community members—and won strong support for the district's efforts. Other options include contributing a regular column to your local newspaper—titled, for example, "Tales From Our Classrooms" or "Character Chronicles"—to which you and others can contribute.

Change How You Run Meetings

Before a meeting, think through the logistics: When and where will it be? What location and type of room best suits the meeting? What materials are needed? What audiovisual or other equipment is required? Will refreshments be available, and if so, what kind? Who needs to be at the meeting? How will you prepare those who are going to be expected to participate?

Begin by building an agenda that advances your objectives and encourages support for your initiatives. Post your agenda one week in advance and give people an opportunity to add their items and begin thinking about yours. Phrase each agenda item so it includes an action verb that describes the outcome you hope to accomplish (make recommendations, identify alternatives, decide on courses of action, discuss, share, etc.). Finally, if you wish, allocate a specific amount of time you will devote to each item (you may find you have too many items for the available time, or the relative time among certain items is inconsistent with your overall priorities).

At the end of each meeting, whether it was with one other person or with 20, take five minutes to collectively summarize what was accomplished and the next steps to be taken. Many administrators find it helpful to take another few minutes to discuss how well you worked together and how you might improve your working relationship in the next meeting.

To help make meetings run more smoothly, designate three roles and what is expected of each:

1. *Recorder*—The recorder takes minutes for the meeting. This person needs to be assertive, check what others have said, and ask for clarification or repetition as needed.

2. *Facilitator*—The facilitator leads the discussion, keeps it focused and headed toward an action agenda, and sticks to the time schedule. The facilitator may be a different person for different agenda items.

3. *Participants*—Participants are all the other people at the meeting. You should set expectations for attendees beyond listening and actively help focus their participation as desired. For example, the facilitator should call for deliberation and input regarding agenda items, and solicit volunteers to be part of any follow-up plans.

After the meeting, send out the minutes with action steps highlighted clearly in bold face or marked in some other way that people will come to recognize.

Rethink Student Assemblies and School Rituals, Celebrations, and Ceremonies

How people come together in a school expresses a great deal about its character. Often, assemblies are meant to inspire or build community among staff and students. For this to happen, assemblies—such as "Peace Symposia," "Justice/Equity Day," black history, Latino heritage, or women's awareness events—should not be isolated, one-shot celebrations. Provide opportunities for prior preparation to set a context for what will happen at the gathering and for inquiry and follow-up questions, rather than static presentation. Follow-up can take place live or via electronic media, distance learning, or the Internet. Doing so will create networks with your local presenters, and help make other presenters who travel to your school more tangible heroes and heroines. More important for your school's character, you will have helped students and staff members come together purposefully and meaningfully to derive individual and collective learning and pride from the assembly experience and its aftermath.

Related to the choice of assembly topics is your choice about what to honor in rituals, ceremonies, or celebrations. Which values in your school are publicly recognized? Examine your yearly cycle of rituals and ceremonies, including assemblies, and classify each one in terms of your priorities. How do you celebrate birthdays of teachers? Other staff? Students? How are other significant personal and professional occurrences in your school recognized? Do you use the public address system, electronic messaging, or school-wide communication systems only for "business," or are they also used to build community? If you find your current practices do not match your priorities, make changes. Add activities that will create a better balance, delete events that do not contribute to your objectives or modify how they are conducted to bring them closer in line with what you are trying to accomplish.

Work with Groups More Effectively and Efficiently

Schools typically have an extensive group structure, both formal and informal. Some groups work together very well over long periods of time and are usually productive. Other groups can't be together for more than a few minutes without some difficulty or conflict arising; they rarely produce worthwhile outcomes. Some groups just exist; no one is quite sure why, or what they do. Researchers have identified two major aspects of group functioning that productive groups demonstrate:

1. Focusing on the task—getting a job done.

2. Focusing on maintenance—keeping the group a cohesive unit regardless of the task.

Groups periodically need to be reminded of their purpose. If no one accepts responsibility for reminding the group it has a task to perform and for refocusing its energies when it strays, the group may drift and never be productive.

Some groups keep changing their expected outcomes over time. They get different assignments, or some jobs are completed and new jobs are identified. If members of the group accept responsibility for their working relationship, then the group will be able to move from task to task without much difficulty. If no one accepts that responsibility and strong negative feelings and conflicts are not addressed, group members may continue to deal with problems generated four tasks ago. Annoyances with past problems or with other group members often prevent them from effectively dealing with the task at hand.

Traditionally, the leader is responsible for being concerned about the group achieving its task or functioning smoothly. A more useful approach is described by the term "distributive leadership." In this approach, all group members accept some responsibility for leadership behaviors, even though one individual may be designated as the person in charge. The research on effective group functioning identifies specific task and maintenance behavior. Task behavior includes such things as clarifying and summarizing group feelings, whereas maintenance behavior deals with encouraging and expressing them (Goleman, 1998). To the extent that group members accept responsibility for demonstrating these behaviors in a group setting, the group can be considered to be effective.

Structured groups often spend time at the end of each meeting summarizing what has been accomplished and what appropriate tasks to act on next. However, effective groups also spend a few minutes at the end of each meeting summarizing and discussing how the group works together. In both cases, the summary activity includes plans for the next meeting. In terms of the task's focus, this means setting an agenda or priorities for the next meeting. In terms of maintenance, this means setting plans for improving the functioning of the group.

The group functions checklist in Figure 9.2 can help you understand the different tasks and roles important to group functioning. As you read through the checklist, think about which roles *you* may fill. Which roles can someone else in the group fill? Which roles are not filled, or filled only sporadically? How might you be more consistent in making sure these latter tasks get done? Much of what takes place in schools occurs in the context of groups (classrooms certainly can and should be thought of as working groups, at least in part, with both task and maintenance functions). Therefore, it is unlikely any social-emotional learning or character education innovations can be sustained in the face of inadequate group process and functioning.

▼ ▼ ▼

Transitions: Review and a Look Ahead

Review

- To turn your good ideas into good realities, you will need to carefully plan your action.
- You can facilitate the action-planning process by thinking about both the details of what needs to be done and how the process unfolds.
- An action-planning process involves a sequence of questions and a series of actions that continually move you and your staff toward meeting your goals and refining your performance.
- A significant and underappreciated part of the action-planning process is anticipating and planning for roadblocks.

Figure 9.2
Group Functions Checklist

TASK FUNCTIONS

1. *Initiating:* Proposing tasks or goals; defining a group problem; suggesting a procedure for solving a problem; suggesting other ideas for consideration.

2. *Information- or opinion-seeking:* Requesting facts on the problem; seeking relevant information; asking for suggestions and ideas.

3. *Information- or opinion-giving:* Offering facts; providing relevant information; stating a belief; giving suggestions or ideas.

4. *Clarifying or elaborating:* Interpreting or reflecting ideas or suggestions; clearing up confusion; indicating alternatives and issues before the group; giving examples.

5. *Summarizing:* Pulling related ideas together; restating suggestions after the group has discussed them.

6. *Consensus-testing:* Sending up "trial balloons" to see if the group is nearing a conclusion or agreement has been reached.

MAINTENANCE FUNCTIONS

1. *Encouraging:* Being friendly, warm, and responsive to others; accepting others and their contributions; listening; showing regard for others by giving them an opportunity or recognition.

2. *Expressing group feelings:* Sensing feeling, mood, and relationships within the group; sharing one's own feelings with other members.

3. *Harmonizing:* Attempting to reconcile disagreements; reducing tension through "pouring oil on troubled waters"; getting people to explore their differences.

4. *Compromising:* Offering to compromise one's own position, ideas, or status; admitting error; disciplining oneself to help maintain the group.

5. *Gate-keeping:* Seeing that others have a chance to speak; keeping the discussion a group discussion rather than allowing one, two, or three people to dominate.

6. *Setting standards:* Expressing standards that will help the group to achieve; applying standards in evaluating group functioning and production.

• Your initial steps should include examining the social-emotional climate around how you invoke heroes and heroines, which stories you tell about your school, how you run meetings, what rituals you have in your school, and how you work with groups.

Bridge

The space between planning and action exists more in tables and flowcharts than it does in reality. Every step you take in preparation for action is already part of the action. At this point, you have mobilized considerable time and energy in your school toward improving your efforts and outcomes in your new initiatives. As you move into a more formal action stage—most typically in the form of a pilot project—you may find it helpful to review the action-research cycle in Appendix C. The procedures in this book have been developed with a focus on creating sustained, institutionalized change, and as such, they may be somewhat different from those you have typically encountered. CASEL, in its focus on implementation for long-term success, identifies certain considerations and choices that can place social-emotional and character programs at the foundation of your school, albeit responsive to changing needs and circumstances. These procedures differ from those previous efforts that have inadvertently led well-intentioned efforts to result in a revolving door of programs and initiatives or something that begins to erode from the moment it is formally initiated. Chapter 10 presents the pathways most used by districts and schools that have made social-emotional and character education approaches an enduring, effective part of their educational routine.

Reflections for Action

• Who have been heroes or heroines in your professional or personal life? What makes these people heroic to you? How do their lessons and examples apply to your school and to bringing social-emotional and character programs to your school?

• What stories do you draw on for inspiration? What opportunities do you have to share these with your staff?

• Thinking about your own experience, for what life decisions do you feel you used an action plan effectively? What decisions could have used a more elaborated action plan? What were the consequences?

• What is your usual emotional response to anticipating road-blocks? What types of roadblocks tend to elicit your strongest negative reactions? How might you best deal with these reactions?

• Where is the opposition to social-emotional learning and character education in your school? What strengths can you mobilize to address this opposition? Compensate for it? Offset it?

• What actions do you most need to take
  – in the next week?
  – in the next two weeks?
  – in the next month?
  – in the next two to three months?
  – in preparation for the end of the school year?
  – in anticipation of the start of the next school year?

▲   ▲   ▲

Learn Constantly:
Obtain Feedback and Modify Accordingly

Feedback is essential for keeping a plan on course. As implementation proceeds, you will need information about its effects on students, staff, parents, and the school as a whole.

Yet, every administrator knows plans are like buoys in waters that are often filled with tricky currents, shifting winds, choppy waves, and the occasional Loch Ness monster. You need many ways to ensure your ship stays on course without undue hardships. Fortunately, you have access to a growing number of techniques that lead to broad involvement in monitoring the implementation plan (whether a pilot or full-scale effort) and in making ongoing course corrections in your social-emotional or character education program.

Tracking Changes

In any change process, it is difficult to monitor your original plans and be professional enough to make changes if they are not working out the way you wanted. Creating a plan or procedure gives you some ideas about what to change if outcomes do not develop as envisioned. Yet, implementing the plan as originally designed cannot become the goal. It is more important to reach the results you want than it is to ensure you execute your initial plan. This is often easier said than done in the politicized world of schools, but keeping an eye on the goal of building students' social-emotional skills and positive character is an ethical responsibility of educational leaders. Furthermore, you can learn about the specific needs of your school by examining the "midcourse corrections" made during implementation. Two aspects of the program's efforts must be monitored to accomplish this—the process used and the outcomes achieved.

Monitoring the Process

The key question for monitoring process involves implementation: What indicators show that individuals are carrying out the intervention as planned? In many of the attempts to change how an organization functions, the primary problem is that the staff are insufficiently trained in the new methods and not given enough time to acclimate to revised expectations. As they try the new ways, they must break old habits and learn new ones. Of course, the process is no different for administrators or anyone else involved.

An excellent approach to dealing with this process is to use the "levels of concern/levels of use," based on the work of Shirley Hord and colleagues (1987) (see Figures 10.1 and 10.2). Their research shows that educators carrying out new programs tend to go through a developmental process to become skilled at what they are doing. During this process, they pass through Hord's two levels.

Typically, it takes two to three years for those carrying out a full-year social-emotional and character education innovation to feel a sense of mastery, which corresponds to the consequences and collaboration levels of concern in Figure 10.1 and the mechanical and routine levels of use in Figure 10.2. It is after this point that the full potential of your work can be realized; staff members are able to mobilize their experience and talent and motivation in the service of improving something they understand, feel comfortable with, and believe in.

As an administrator, you are very likely going through the same developmental progression. Try to conceptualize implementation as a continuing process or cycle, or, as one administrator, Thomas Schuyler of New Jersey, has shared at numerous workshops, an ongoing sea voyage or series of voyages. The levels of use and concern of your staff (or crew) will have important ramifications as you take each step in carrying out your school or district plans for social-emotional learning and character education. Crew members need to learn their individual tasks, gradually come together to coordinate their efforts on the ship, and then look to make refinements to get even better results with the same or less effort. The captain of the ship obviously does not work the same way with an experienced crew as with a novice crew; as the crew gets better, it is possible to take on more challenging voyages. Certainly, taking on a highly challenging voyage in stormy, poorly charted seas with an inexperienced crew is not a good idea. As Schuyler has said, in such situations, captains (administrators) need to be prepared for their ship to become a submarine because there is a great likelihood of taking on significant water.

The levels of concern and levels of use indicate a different need being expressed by staff in their quest to reach a level of comfort and skill with social-emotional programs. In a way, each level represents a new problem to be solved

Figure 10.1

Individuals' Level of Concern About a Social Emotional Learning and Character Education Innovation

Level of concern provides you with a way to keep track of staff members' attitudes and aspirations as they carry out social-emotional learning and character education efforts over time.

Level of Concern	Definition and Indicator
Awareness	The extent to which an individual knows about social-emotional learning and character education and believes it is a matter of importance for his or her job role, task performance, or overall school and students' success. The initial level of concern is represented by the statement, "I am not concerned about social-emotional learning."
Informational	The extent to which someone would like to know more about social-emotional learning and character education. The initial level of concern is represented by the statement, "I would like to know more."
Personal	The extent to which someone begins to consider the personal impact of carrying out a social-emotional or character innovation, or of *not* carrying it out. Having a personal concern follows after acquiring information or training. The initial level of concern is represented by the statement, "How will it affect me and the work I do?"
Management	The extent to which a person is grappling with the logistics of carrying out a social-emotional or character innovation. Management concerns are greatest during the initial start-up and when significant changes in the school are made, whether or not they are program-related. The initial level of concern is represented by the statement, "I am concerned about my ability to manage everything that the innovation seems to require of me."

Figure 10.1 (*Continued*)

Level of Concern	Definition and Indicator
Consequences	The extent to which someone is focused on the impact of social-emotional learning on students and how to maximize it. Once an innovation has settled into routine use and people are comfortable with its mechanics, they usually turn their concerns toward its impact. The initial level of concern is represented by the statement, "How is the innovation impacting students and how can I improve it and excite students about it?"
Collaboration	The extent to which a person recognizes the greatest accomplishments occur through the coordinated and synergistic efforts of many people in the school. After establishing a level of confidence and competence with their own role in carrying out the innovation, some people recognize that social-emotional learning and character education are a process of skill and character development that requires coordination and continuity over time. The initial level of concern is represented by the statement, "I would like to coordinate my effort with others to maximize the impact of the innovation."
Refocusing	The extent to which, based on experience with implementation of the program, some one begins to integrate his or her own ideas about what might improve the effort. The initial level of concern is represented by the statement, "I would like to work on supplementing, enhancing, and making this innovation better."

Figure 10.2
Individuals' Level of Use of the Social-Emotional Learning and Character Education Innovation

Level of use provides you with a framework to evaluate the extent to which people are doing their part in the action plan. Applying the level of use perceptively requires you to understand individuals' prior experience with social-emotional program implementation and the extent to which they are receiving training and supervision in the effort being carried out in your school.

Level	Definition and Implementation Implications
Non-use	Staff at this level display little or no knowledge, no involvement, and no actions to help them become involved. This level may reflect lack of training or exposure, or unwillingness or hesitation to carry out what is expected. You need to determine the particular barrier to use and provide what is needed by way of skill or incentive.
Orientation	At this level, staff have acquired or are acquiring information about social-emotional learning and character education and its value orientation and what it will require to carry out the innovation. To move ahead, staff need introductory information about specific program goals, requirements, and time lines; be careful not to overwhelm them with too much information or to set expectations too high.
Preparation	Staff at this level are clearly preparing to use a new social-emotional or character idea or process. They need concrete information on what the innovation will look like, what materials they will use, and how to prepare themselves to take the first steps in getting started.
Mechanical use	At this level, staff are focusing on short-term, day-to-day use. They are working on mastering the specific tasks and techniques they must carry out. What they are doing may appear disjointed or superficial, and may look this way for one or two years, though gradual improvement, comfort, and fluidity should be noticed. To help them move ahead, staff need support for trouble-shooting implementation. This can take many forms (e.g., observing other teachers, additional consultation or supervision, e-mail contact with experts, peer-group meetings to share and learn).

Figure 10.2 (*Continued*)

Level	Definition and Implementation Implications
Routine	At this level, use of the innovation is established. Regular patterns of implementation predominate and few changes are made in ongoing use. Those working at this level are best supported by praise and recognition for what they are doing; however, be sure to check to see if there is any need for assistance in making implementation easier or better.
Refinement	Staff at this level begin to fine tune their own program work and the work of their most immediate collaborators based on feedback from consumers and clients and from their own experience. This is an inevitable and positive development. The challenge for administrators is to provide support and reinforcement for innovation while maintaining the core aspects of the plan.
Integration	At the integration level, staff begin to step back and look at the big picture of the program work they are doing. They focus on how to combine their own efforts with those of colleagues. To help foster integration, you should support naturally occurring interactions and collaborations, and plan contexts in which cooperation can occur.
Renewal	Staff at this level are interested in reevaluating how to best reach the program's goals in a high-quality manner. They are using the innovation at a high level of skill, with integration, but changes in population, student needs, staffing patterns, freshness and relevance of materials, or other concerns appear to call for modification in the spirit of maintaining or improving effectiveness. It is not unusual at this level to see key staff members independently explore ways to improve the system in place. You can help channel new ideas into improved implementation by supporting this exploration and by providing opportunities for staff to share and discuss desirable, coordinated changes in the school's social-emotional efforts.

Source: Data from Hord et al. (1987). *Taking charge of change.* Alexandria, VA: Association for Supervision and Curriculum Development.

using the steps in social decision-making and social problem solving presented in Figure 1.1.

Monitoring Outcomes

Of course, the point of improving the implementation process is to improve the outcome. Therefore, you will need a methodology for monitoring the extent to which you are meeting your goals, or at least reaching various benchmarks of progress along the way. Usually, educators depend on year-end evaluations to determine the degree of success. That is too long to wait when you are installing a new program and introducing serious changes. Develop data-gathering techniques that produce formative information on a daily, weekly, and monthly basis. The simplest involves a checklist of the frequency of targeted, observed behavior, such as decreases in conflicts, absenteeism, lateness, or referrals, and increases in helping behaviors, participation in extracurricular activities, or use of social graces. The actual list you develop will grow naturally from your planning processes as you identify criteria for success in your efforts. You and your staff must know what progress looks like, which takes the form of answers to these questions:

- How will you know when things are getting better?
- What are the indicators you look at that tell you progress is being made?
- What will it look like when you are mostly successful? Fully successful? How will you know? What will you see?

Outcomes can be thought about in terms of two domains: effect and satisfaction. Each is represented by a key question: What indicators show that the desired outcome in students is taking place? What indicators show the extent to which constituents of social-emotional efforts (recipients, implementers, others in the school, parents, etc.) are satisfied with what is taking place?

Examples of Monitoring Methods

For both of these domains, you may already be collecting data, either formally or informally, that can be used to monitor effect and satisfaction. You may need to collect additional assessments to help monitor implementation.

Monitoring implementation. You likely already have your teachers' lesson plans. Consider making social-emotional learning and character education part of their formal classroom observation agenda. Let staff know you will be dropping in on social-emotional and character education classroom activities. Have teachers report on the initiative at staff meetings. Gather records with regard to school-wide implementation. Maurice Elias, a co-author of this book, worked with one school in Plainfield, New Jersey, to carry out a school-wide program of positive recognition. To provide an indicator of implementation, a large poster was created and on it, each class periodically listed the amount of positive recognition dispensed. (In this particular program, staff members awarded children who took positive action a form of locally created currency, which they could redeem individually and as classes.) Having such a public record ensured visibility to classes that were not doing their fair share of dispensing.

Monitoring effect. School records—such as the number of disciplinary actions taken and ratings on the "other side of the report card" about behavior in groups, cooperation, absences, lateness, misbehavior, and the like—are all useful. Some schools implementing programs have changed their report cards and progress report formats to incorporate specific behavioral indicators related to social-emotional or character goals or benchmarks of progress. Behavioral rating scales, such as the teacher-child rating scale (Hightower et al., 1986) and the social skills rating scale (Gresham & Elliott, 1990) can also be useful. Though they are labor-intensive, they are normed and psychometrically reliable and valid, and can be useful for annual or biennial monitoring at alternate grade levels (e.g., assess every year or every other year at grades 1, 3, 5, 7, 9, 11, or at other strategic times depending on the configuration of your schools).

Monitoring satisfaction. This area is often the most neglected. Yet, research and common sense make it clear that staff will not implement something well if they do not like it, and students will have a very hard time learning in a context they detest. Particularly for social-emotional efforts, there is no reason to carry out something that is perceived as a burden. There are far too many approaches to choose from that have proved highly satisfactory to implementers and recipients. Find ways to get feedback from teachers, parents, and students on what they like most and least, what they find effective, what they see being put to use in a general way, and how they feel about specific components of the approach being carried out. Formats for consumer feedback can be found in Elias and Tobias (1996) and Elias (1993).

Form a Coordinating Committee

One option existing at the cusp of monitoring process and outcomes is putting in place some ongoing quality control procedures. Both CASEL and CEP find that schools and districts that have carried out social-emotional programs effectively for long periods of time have evolved a structure consisting of a committee or other kind of working group that coordinates the program activities in a school (Elias et al., 1997). A committee often gives important visibility and sanction to the work being done and provides a vehicle for coordinating efforts with other aspects of the school curriculum. This can be especially important when your school is implementing a whole-school reform model and must abide by certain constraints. Sometimes, elementary and secondary school committees are necessary within a district. The kinds of duties involved can be inferred from a sample "job description" provided by the social development coordinator of The Children's Institute, Verona, New Jersey, in Figure 10.3.

Figure 10.3
Activities of a Social Development Coordinator

1. Organize and implement structural framework of the school-wide program

    – create and maintain a skills chart showing what everyone is focusing on
    – arrange regular staff sharing meetings
    – organize and maintain lesson binders
    – convene a social development committee
    – post classroom instructional schedules
    – check to see if posters with social-emotional and character education terminology are widely posted

2. Train new and current staff members

    – plan and conduct orientation and follow-up
    – arrange as needed advanced social-emotional and character education workshops and collaborations
    – find times for staff to learn from one another

3. Extend the program into the children's homes

    – arrange regular parent workshops
    – organize a social-emotional and character education family Learn-A-Thon
    – compile and distribute information booklets on social-emotional learning and character education
    – coordinate social development newsletters (staff and students)
    – host a Social Development Day at the school for families

4. Motivate staff

    – minimize paperwork
    – implement program in existing curriculum
    – keep exciting materials available
    – get staff involved

▼　▼　▼

Transitions: Review and a Look Ahead

Review

• Feedback about how your efforts are being implemented and about the outcome of your efforts is essential for long-term progress.

• Carrying out a program with skill and confidence is a developmental process that takes staff members two to three years in most instances.

• To monitor implementation, focus on the levels of concern staff have about social-emotional learning and character education and the innovations you are proposing, and on the levels to which they put the innovations to practical use as part of their everyday routines.

• Identify specific indicators that tell you and various staff members the extent to which progress is made and goals reached.

Bridge

At this point, your initiative is clearly under way and you are into the complex art of navigation. At all points along the journey, it is important that you remain in close touch with your mentor and other administrators who are taking similar journeys. Your experience, as well as the research literature, tells you plans are really rolling plans, because they are in a constant state of reevaluation and modification. Few things are planned more meticulously—with incredible teamwork, coordination, communication, and constant feedback—than NASA missions. Yet, as we all know, the primary strength of the NASA team is its ability to solve problems on the fly. That's why you may find it helpful to go back to Figure 1.1 and use the social decision-making and problem-solving process to help you address the various glitches and opportunities that are sure to present themselves over time. As your efforts proceed, you will find your staff developing more expertise, and this will allow for wonderful creativity, accomplishment, and the meeting of your greatest challenges. However, it is important for you not to push your staff beyond their capabilities during their trip through the stages of becoming skilled program implementers. Chapter 11 addresses some of the ways to cultivate leadership and expertise and create a learning community for social-emotional learning and character education that will sustain and enhance your school's work and mobilize collective skill and resources to address problems that arise.

Reflections for Action

- Think about times you learned a new professional skill or procedure, or brought a new program into your school. How did it feel at first? How long did it take to feel comfortable with what you were doing? How long before you had a sense of mastery?

- What do you feel are the best indicators of the social-emotional or character status of your students? Your staff? How can you better collect information to help use these indicators as a barometer of progress?

- How might you solicit opinions about and gauge satisfaction with your program from constituencies in your school other than staff, such as students, parents, school board members, and members of the general community?

- Whom might you want to select for a coordinating committee? Who might lead it? How would you view your role?

Look to the Future:
Cultivate Participation and Leadership to Build
and Sustain a Caring Community of Learners

The ultimate goal of any change process is to shape the school or organization into a learning organization. When a school is a learning organization, its leadership and staff are eager to understand how well it is accomplishing its various goals. They use this knowledge in a spirit of continuous improvement to better reach goals and include all children. When social-emotional learning and character education are brought into a school in a systematic way, the school becomes a particular kind of learning organization: a caring community of learners. All learning organizations use regularly collected data to monitor and adjust their programs as needed. But a caring community of learners also focuses on how the insights gained through implementing social-emotional innovations can apply to the way adults and students treat each other as they deal with individual and collective issues.

As you lead your school toward becoming a learning organization, you need to recognize the operation of strong, systemic forces. These forces act on all programs and initiatives, regardless of topic or content. You must carefully account for these systemic forces because they have such a strong effect on the feelings of students and staff. Among the most important lessons staff members need to learn is how much their efforts are interrelated. Everyone's small—or not so small—part of the program is essential for your innovations to succeed. As your staff comes to understand this and work together more closely, the combination of their greater collaboration and the social-emotional and character instruction being provided to students creates a crucible from which a strong, sustainable caring community of learners can emerge. Figure 11.1 outlines one useful way of looking at the systemic nature of change in schools and how this links to schools' functioning as learning organizations. It is derived from the extensive administrative consultation experience of one of this book's authors, Bernard Novick.

Create Channels and Opportunities for Communication

Perhaps the least discussed yet most vital element of a learning organization that strives to be a caring community of learners is communication. Because of the systemic nature of change, your school will function best when its various parts and constituencies know what the others are doing, the problems they are encountering, the variations they are attempting, and the questions they are asking. Your success in administering social-emotional and character initiatives depends on you well you convince your staff that they need to share information and bring concerns to the surface. One

---

Figure 11.1
Novick's Principles of Systems, Systemic Change, and
Learning Organizations

• A system is a collection of component parts, people, and programs that includes a feedback loop that uses outcome data to reinforce or modify the interaction.

• The system in place is perfectly designed to give you the results you are getting.

• If you are not satisfied with the results you are getting now, you must change your system to one that gets you the results you want.

• Systemic change is a term that describes efforts focused on changing the systems in place for systems that produce the wanted results. In most cases, it is used to describe changing an unconscious system of discrete individuals and activities working for unclear or unknown purposes into a combined, integrated group of people and activities working toward shared purposes and goals.

• The process of systemic change begins with developing a working vision and mission and set of values for the system. Then identify the component parts that must be integrated. Next you must design a process for aligning these various discrete components to the point where they work together in support of each other toward the achievement of shared and agreed upon vision, mission, and values.

• A process is a group of tasks or activities designed to generate a specific outcome.

• A high-performing learning organization is one where any members or activities within the system can demonstrate how they are contributing toward the achievement of the system's purposes or goals. Further, they can show how they interact with other constituent or component elements of the system to work together towards that end.

• The last step in becoming a learning organization (or an organization that learns) is to build in procedures for ensuring that the system stays on course in light of changing conditions.

---

of the reasons for using a problem-solving process to plan and initiate programs is to create a problem-solving mentality among your staff and establish structures and procedures for sharing and communicating that will continue after implementation begins.

Here are some excellent ways to communicate with your staff and the school community:

- Allocate general faculty meeting time for your new social-emotional program.
- Ensure it is in teacher plan books.
- Require that staff members discuss the program at grade level, content area, or departmental faculty meetings.
- Assign responsibility for making the program visually prominent in the school, via bulletin boards, dedicated walls, artwork, collages of accomplishments, etc.
- Put the program on the agenda of the homeschool or parent-teacher association.
- Communicate your initiative regularly to the school board, your administrative teams, and local media outlets.

Create a Vital Learning Organization

A series of leadership tasks are considered hallmarks of schools that function as learning organizations with a high degree of emotional intelligence and sound character. These tasks are ongoing, and although they are ultimately the responsibility of top administrators, they are most effective when many members of the school community participate in them. By empowering staff to become meaningfully involved in the leadership of your school and in sustaining change, you create a stronger, more stable school climate. Your efforts become less dependent on the presence of a limited number of specific people, including yourself. You are, in essence, using your leadership skills and the systemic nature of change to design a system that will produce the desired results for your initiative, even while personnel, students, and, even the desired results change.

Here is a list of key leadership tasks:

- **Set clear goals.** Maintain, periodically review, and update school goals.
- **Cultivate self-assessment.** As you monitor the program, shift more responsibility to those carrying out the work.
- **Deliver feedback with care.** Ask yourself, "What do I want to teach and how can I convey feedback in a way that will stimulate a desire to improve?"
- **Build skills.** Take the time to train in detail; the more skillful people are, the more your school can do.
- **Provide models.** We can best draw inspiration and techniques from what we see in action, or participate in. Arrange for staff to see social-emotional learning and character education programs in another school.
- **Encourage practice.** Begin with pilot projects and give people time to learn what they are eventually going to be expected to do. Respect the time needed to learn.
- **Arrange support.** Everybody benefits from a mentor and from contact with a community of peers who are learning together and exchanging ideas and reflecting on their learning.
- **Encourage and reinforce learning.** Don't take learning for granted. Formal and informal encouragement and reinforcement increase the desire to learn and improve.
- **Make change self-directed.** Encourage everyone to have personal and organizational goals and to monitor their progress on both.
- **Give performance feedback.** Periodically and clearly, let members of your organization know what you think about what they are doing, where they stand with you, and what you think they might aspire to.

- **Expect and prevent relapse.** All learning involves ups and downs, especially when changing old habits. Some of these old habits include hiding problems or concerns, avoiding difficulties, resisting modifications to plans in response to obstacles, and giving up. Make it clear that your school intends to leave these habits behind.

▼   ▼   ▼

Transitions: Review and a Look Ahead

Ultimately, the successful, long-term implementation of social-emotional learning and character education involves establishing a learning organization that is a caring community of learners. No approach, program, or effort is static. Yet, few effective changes are whims or fads. The best way to ground changes is in the documented experience of your own organization in meeting needs and attaining objectives. As populations, resources, constraints, and knowledge change, so must social-emotional and character education efforts in a school. Of course, this is true in every aspect of education. And as schools become more effective learning organizations, the synergy of operating across areas in the spirit of continuous improvement will enrich your efforts. That, in turn, will make all other aspects of the school—including genuine achievement and deep learning in academics—more likely.

As you look ahead, you will no doubt see the increased challenges that face our educational system in the coming decades. Society is undergoing change at a rapid rate. Technology is affecting both the process of learning and the learners themselves. Family life is not what it was one, two, or three decades ago; it is essential to understand and work with changing trends in family life. Teaching is highly challenging and rewarding; being an educational leader has the potential to be even more so. As noted earlier, caring relationships form the foundation of all lasting learning. By nurturing relationships in the context of a caring community that is also a learning organization, you will be able to cope with changes while not sacrificing the interpersonal ties that are so important for students, staff, parents, and the community. A growing number of schools are meeting the challenge of integrating high standards of academics and social-emotional programs. There is no reason yours cannot be among them.

Reflections for Action

As you move your school toward becoming a caring community of learners, continually reflect on the presence of features that sustain people in starting and maintaining social-emotional and character programs in schools. These are listed below. The opposite of these features inhibits people from working with the social-emotional and character approach. To what extent are the following features present among staff and volunteers in your school? How can you strengthen them?

- They feel pride in what they are doing.
- They believe they are taking actions that link with their value systems.
- They possess positive energy and a positive sense of well-being.
- They have the skills necessary to carry out program activities.
- They discover they have a lot to contribute to the character and climate of the school.
- They realize their own individual work in the program is part of a larger movement toward the same goals.
- They feel a sense of civic responsibility.
- They experience deep dissatisfaction with problems that children experience.
- They have confidence their efforts will create a better world for those they care about.

▲   ▲   ▲

Epilogue:
A Farewell from Bernard Novick

Bernard Novick—the inspiration behind this book and the person whose experience as an educational administrator provides its base for practice—did not live to see its completion. In the draft, however, even before he realized that he had a life-threatening illness, Bernie wanted to reach out to readers, to let his fellow administrators know that he "walked the talk" and that he would be available to help them implement social-emotional learning and character education. Why? Bernie cared deeply about children and schools—he loved both and wanted nothing less than the best for both. He was a deep believer in total quality and total caring. His wife, Phyllis Novick, remembered this when she accepted our invitation to share some thoughts about Bernie.

It's difficult to separate Bernie, the educator, from Bernie the person," she said. "He automatically taught almost every waking minute. It was like breathing to him, a reflex. Everything he read or experienced seemed to be stored in his brain and would come out at the right moment with the right connection to other bits of information stored there so that it fit the need of the situation. No one ever spent 5 minutes with Bernie without learning something....

For me, the key skill Bernie had as an educator was empowerment," she continued. "He had a way of giving everyone unconditional positive regard that made the person feel accepted and important. He made people feel they could do anything and he had the skills to show them how to do it in a low-key, nonthreatening way. He helped his students (by that I mean anyone he met) discover the answers for themselves so that they felt the solution came from them, so they 'owned' the solution. He was the supreme enabler in the most positive sense of the word.

We learned a lot from his wisdom and our years of collaboration. Although Bernie cannot carry out his pledge of personal support, he will always provide inspiration. We remain committed to provide the support Bernie had planned with *kavanah*, which is a Hebrew word meaning deep, spiritual, focused, intentional and dedicated attention and effort. Bernie's message follows.

A Final Word

As an educator, I not only wanted my students to master skills and acquire knowledge, but just as importantly, I wanted them to master a process they could use and apply in their lives and continued learning. This book is presented in that light. It contains knowledge and processes, skill and content. Its purpose is not only to help you install a social-emotional learning program, but also to feel comfortable with a process you can apply to other issues in your school and in your life.

We would like to hear from you as you progress in this journey.

—Bernie

Appendix A

Social and Emotional Learning 101: An Introduction to Basic Principles

Social and emotional learning can be seen as an educational application of emotional intelligence theory. Many researchers have attempted to delineate various dimensions of emotional intelligence. By far, the most popular are the five areas of emotional intelligence presented in detail by Dan Goleman in *Emotional Intelligence* (1995) and by Elias, Tobias, and Friedlander (1999, 2000) in *Emotionally Intelligent Parenting* and *Raising Emotionally Intelligent Teenagers*. The skill components of emotional intelligence, when applied in an educational context, provide a framework for understanding the basic principles of social-emotional learning. These components are summarized here.

1. Awareness of One's Own Feelings and Those of Others.

Definition. People who can reflect on and accurately label their feelings find themselves at a distinct social, academic, and vocational advantage. Meanwhile, those who cannot distinguish, for example, being bored from being mad, upset from sad, or glad from proud, will wind up acting inappropriately in many situations. Evidence even suggests that students who commit acts of extreme violence could have disordered emotional functioning. These young people seem to have deficiencies in recognizing the signs of feelings in others and knowing how to accurately label them.

Applications. Knowing when to ask a teacher for an extension or when to ask someone for a date are matters of considerable practical significance to many students. We can and must teach students the skills of social literacy. Particularly in low literacy environments, students who do not understand the nuances of social interaction can fail to pick up subtleties in what they are reading. This emotional domain is perhaps most relevant when you are hiring new staff, since this is such a basic people skill.

2. Empathy and Understanding Others' Points of View.

Definition. Empathy is the capacity to share in another's feelings. It is related, of course, to being aware of both your own feelings and those of others. Even more related is being able to know how another person sees something. Indeed, empathy is seeing something through another's eyes or, as the sage Hillel said centuries ago, "Do not judge others until you stand in their shoes." Though difficult to do, understanding other people's points of view *and* their feelings about what is happening is a big part of what defines us as human beings.

Empathy requires skills in careful listening as well as reading the nonverbal body language and tone of voice that often convey more than our words—in essence, it is a nonverbal emotional understanding of others. But it also involves other skills. Cognitive ability matters, as does range of life experiences. People who have grown up with television, movies, videos, and the Internet tend to draw on these media as "reality" without regard to the life experiences of their creators.

Applications. Many teens act more mature than they truly are—perhaps they are exposed to so many life experiences in a shallow and impersonal way, thanks to television and videos. Sadly, the same can be true for some of your younger staff members and parents. Young children (and immature adults) tend to view the world through their own wants and needs. As kids get older, around 7 or 8 years of age, they become better able to negotiate, compromise, and be tolerant. Do your staff members show those same three traits? It depends on their experiences in understanding others' perspectives. Service opportunities—for both staff and students—are among the most valuable and potent ways to build empathy and understanding. We need to look for ways to encourage such opportunities.

3. Self-Control and Adherence to the 24 Karat Golden Rule of Education.

Definition. Healthier and more successful students and staff are those who are able to control their impulses to go after immediate rewards. The Marshmallow Test, as recounted by Dan Goleman in *Emotional Intelligence* (1995), provides an excellent illustration. Researchers conducted an experiment in which young children were told they would be left alone and if they wanted to, they could have the marshmallow on the table in front of them. *But*, if they waited until a researcher came back into the room, they could have *two* marshmallows. Impulsiveness on even this simple test was associated with relatively poor results on a variety of psychological and behavioral indicators. Most remarkable is that years later, the less impulsive students did 200 points better on their SATs, the scholastic aptitude tests so important for college entry.

Why does this impulsive behavior rob students of academic success and staff of vocational success? A moment's reflection is all that is necessary to understand. Too little patience with what it takes to undertake projects seriously and in-depth; too little discipline to prepare properly, like

110

carefully reading all the choices and questions on the exam and related materials—social and emotional skills are intertwined with academic outcomes in many ways.

Applications. Today's sped-up culture pushes students to develop habits of moving quickly, looking less carefully, waiting for shorter periods, and being less patient. These tendencies are both subtle and pervasive; many of your newer staff members also have been socialized for speed. As challenges are faced and frustrations mount, it is essential for you as an administrator to have good social-emotional insight into yourself and others and to try to "keep your cool."

What is the 24 Karat Golden Rule of Education? "Do unto your students as you would have other people do unto *your own* children." We came up with this variation of the original Golden Rule—"Do unto others as you would have others do unto you,"—because we need to apply it to schooling today. With life as hectic and stressed as it is, many administrators, in a moment of honest reflection, may recall times when they have said and done things to their students or staff that they are not especially proud of. The 24 Karat Golden Rule asks that you take your students' and staff members' perspectives with empathy; control your own impulses; know when you are overwhelmed; and stop yourself from taking it out on others. Easy to say, very hard to do.

It can help to look at people in a way that keeps their strengths in mind. See their best possibilities and speak to them as if those possibilities are fragile and might not come to pass if your confidence in them seems shaky.

We can justify the 24 Karat Golden Rule of Education in other ways, as well. Strong anger, frustration, anxiety, sadness, and similar emotions interfere with people's learning and performance. In particular, students have a hard time learning from people who say hurtful things about them or their classmates, regardless of how outstanding those people may be as educators. The stress and pace of life may lead to momentary lapses in judgment and control. Ensuring that everyone in your school is encouraged to use—and be recognized for—valued strengths will prepare them for those lapses from others and cushion their effect. Then, both staff and students will be more able to manage impulsive behavior, relate positively to others individually and in groups, and develop empathy and the ability to take others' perspectives. These skills are essential to academic, career, and life advancement.

4. Positive Attitude and Orientation Toward Goals and Plans.

Definition. More and more literature suggests hopefulness and positive spirits have a distinct biochemistry, including improved blood flow, cardiovascular and aerobic efficiency, immune system activity, and stress-level reduction. Laughter is linked to our creativity and inventiveness, and these, of course, are linked to the ability to be clear about goals, solve problems in new ways, and make plans to see our ideas realized. An emerging discipline of positive psychology is founded on these beliefs, as well as a professional organization, the American Association for Therapeutic Humor (http://www.aath.org). Having a positive attitude is also essential to learning effectively in today's stressful society.

Applications. Maintaining a positive attitude may sometimes seem like a monumental task, especially at the end of a long workweek. Practicing this skill, however, can benefit you and your staff in terms of increased physical and mental well being. Are you able to stay goal-oriented and avoid the tendency to point fingers and let problems derail your plans? Are you setting goals wisely, and do your plans reach them? Students and staff need more help than ever in organizing to get their work done, and done well (not just gotten "out of the way").

5. Use of BEST Social Skills in Handling Relationships.

Definition: BEST, an acronym for effective assertive communication (Elias & Clabby, 1998), stands for the following:

Body posture
Eye contact
Saying the right words (or skipping the wrong words)
Tone of voice

Communication goes beyond what you say and includes the approach you take and the care you show your listener. Though differing cultural factors define, more or less, appropriate ways to do things, there are some actions that are sure to turn students off, regardless of their culture and the context.

Applications: Do you do any of these?

- **Body**: Position yourself in a way that is challenging, disinterested, or not facing others when speaking.
- **Eyes**: Roll your eyes in disbelief.
- **Speech**: Call people by a name they don't like or talk about them in the third person even when they are present for the conversation ("Maybe Steven needs to learn how to study better." "I am sitting right here, and I hate to study. I know how, I just think it's a waste.").
- **Tone**: Speak in a sarcastic, bossy, demanding, or condescending manner.

When you are at your BEST, you are like a car with new radial tires. You are right on top of your conversations and interactions, gripping every curve and responding smoothly to every bump. You convey to other people that you respect them and want to be there with them, communicating meaningfully.

Another way to put BEST skills to work is to use them when you work with a group. As an administrator, you want your faculty to function well as a group. This will happen to the extent they not only carry out their basic assignments but also feel they contribute to the betterment of the school and to the life of the surrounding community. Certain skills are necessary for this, and not all staff members possess them. Learning to listen to others carefully and accurately, to take turns, to harmonize different feelings, to compromise, to create consensus, and to state your ideas clearly are among many social-emotional skills that help people work better in groups. Having faculty model these skills and values also goes a long way to teaching similar ones to your students-at least as much as any formal curriculum could, especially as students move to the secondary school years.

Summary

Emotions strongly affect how and what students learn in school and beyond. Positive emotions and feelings of being appreciated for valued strengths can be very motivating. Social and emotional learning asks you to focus on others' strengths while also building needed skills to manage impulsive behavior, relate positively to others individually and in groups, and develop empathy and the ability to take others' perspectives. These competencies underlie success in all human endeavors and most certainly are vital to academic, career, civic, and life advancement.

Appendix B

Social-Emotional Learning and Character Education: An Overview of Principles

Social and emotional skills underlie successful everyday interpersonal interactions across a range of settings (see Appendix A for an explication of principles based on the seminal work of Daniel Goleman). "Character" is a concept with many definitions. A common view is that a person of character lives his or her life in a principled, ethical manner, and that doing so requires social-emotional learning skills. CEP articulates a set of principles to guide schools in implementing character education initiatives (see Figure B.1). Also, CASEL identifies a set of guidelines schools can use to increase the likelihood that students will develop social and emotional skills. Although the CEP and CASEL approaches draw from different backgrounds, they share important traits. Both recommend high-quality, yearlong initiatives that are continuous within a given year; ideally, these efforts continue over several years and have many components.

Being familiar with these two sets of ideas allows administrators to draw from both points of view and to link efforts with both groups. This is particularly important because your constituents—parents, local politicians, and teachers—may be more familiar with one set of ideas than another.

CASEL identifies 39 guidelines supported by research and practice as instrumental in bringing about lasting, effective social-emotional programs and practices in schools.

Contained in *Promoting Social and Emotional Learning: Guidelines for Educators* (Elias et al., 1997), these guidelines can be seen as a complement to the character education principles. The following is a summary of the CASEL guidelines:

- Build and reinforce life skills and social competencies, health-promotion and problem-prevention skills, coping skills and social support for transitions and crises, and positive contributory service.

Figure B.1
Principles of Character Education

1. Character Education promotes core ethical values as the basis of good character.

2. "Character" must be comprehensively defined to include thinking, feeling, and behavior.

3. Effective Character Education requires an intentional, proactive, and comprehensive approach that promotes the core values in all phases of school life.

4. The school must be a caring community.

5. To develop character, students need opportunities for moral action.

6. Effective Character Education includes a meaningful and challenging academic curriculum that respects all learners and helps them.

7. Character Education should strive to develop students' intrinsic motivation.

8. The school staff must become a learning and moral community in which all share responsibility for character education and attempt to adhere to the same core values.

9. Character Education requires moral leadership from both staff and students.

10. The school must recruit parents and community members as full partners in the character-building effort.

11. Evaluation of Character Education should assess the character of the school, the school staff's functioning as character educators, and the extent to which students manifest good character.

Source: Lickona, T., Schaps, E., and Lewis, C. (1995). *Eleven Principles of Effective Character Education.* Washington, DC: Character Education Partnership.

- Link efforts to build social and emotional skills to developmental milestones and to the need to help students cope with ongoing life events and local circumstances.
- Emphasize the promotion of prosocial attitudes and values about self, others, work, and citizenship.
- Integrate social-emotional learning with traditional academics to enhance learning in both areas.
- Build a caring, supportive, and challenging classroom and school climate to assure effective social-emotional teaching and learning.
- Provide social-emotional learning through multimodal instruction including modeling, role-playing, prompting performance, feedback, open-ended questioning, reinforcement in all aspects of school life, and attention to both the cognitive and affective states of learners.
- Integrate and coordinate programs and activities with the regular curriculum and life of the classroom and school.
- Foster enduring and pervasive effects through collaboration between home and school.

Looking at the CEP principles and then at these guidelines may leave you with a strong sense of déjà vu, because differences in terminology and language mask deep similarities (see Figure B.2). For example, compare the two CEP principles in the left column of the figure with the CASEL guidelines in the right. The remaining CEP principles and CASEL guidelines show similar overlaps.

The Character Education principles and CASEL guidelines clearly converge. This can best be illustrated by looking at the features found in schools that have earned the designation National Schools of Character (Farmer, 1999):

- Approved/recognized curriculum-based instruction in standards for enacting sound interpersonal behavior.

Figure B.2
Character Education Partnership Principles vs. Collaborative for Academic, Social, and Emotional Learning Guidelines

Character Education Principles	Corresponding SEL Guidelines
Principle 1: CE promotes core ethical values as the basis of good character.	Guideline 3: SEL programs emphasize the promotion of prosocial values about self, others and work.
Principle 3: Effective character education requires an intentional, proactive, and comprehensive approach that promotes the core values in all phases of school life.	Guideline 1: Educators at all levels need explicit plans to help students become knowledgeable, responsible, and caring. Guideline 4: It is most beneficial to provide a developmentally appropriate combination of formal, curriculum-based instruction with ongoing, informal, and infused opportunities to develop social and emotional skills from preschool through high school. Guideline 10: The integration of SEL with traditional academics greatly enhances learning in both areas.

Source: Lickona, T., Schaps, E., and Lewis, C. (1995). *Eleven Principles of Effective Character Education.* Washington, DC: Character Education Partnership.

- Teacher training in theory and instruction supporting the instruction cited above.
- Core values, themes are enacted throughout the curriculum.
- Positive recognition/student appreciation.
- Schoolwide commitment to nonviolence/bully prevention/peacemaking.
- Attention paid to start-of-day and end-of-day transitions/morning meetings/greetings/sharing circles.

- Advisories/group guidance.
- Ethical discussions/classroom-based conflict resolution.
- Reflection-oriented community service/service learning experience.
- Problem solving/think time/caring room.
- Student contracts/honor code/school rules/classroom constitutions emphasizing caring, responsibility, respect.
- Acts of kindness.
- Peer leadership classes.
- Techniques for self-discipline and self-control.
- Parenting skills classes and internships.
- Positive staff modeling of behaviors of sound interpersonal skills.
- Homeschool partnerships.
- School newsletters for students, staff, and parents.

Schools recognized by CEP and those viewed by CASEL as "flagship schools" have at least one of the preceding features; the vast majority have schoolwide components that continue through the year and contribute in a substantial way to the schools' climate. The clear convergence of social-emotional learning and character education allows administrators great flexibility in putting together cohesive and comprehensive initiatives that fit with efforts already underway in your school or district.

Appendix C

An Overview of the Action-Research Cycle

If, in the process of trying something new, you ask yourself, "How did it work, and how would I do it differently next time?" then you have already used a key principle of action-research—a powerful tool that shapes the process of program implementation so "practitioners [can] seek to effect transformations in their own practices" (Brown & Dowling, 1998, p. 152). It is a methodology that many educators use intuitively, at least in a rudimentary form.

Formalizing the process for the purposes of school-based program implementation can prove helpful for several reasons. First, given the already considerable demands on your time and energy, it is all too easy to abandon the action-research process and use an approach of, "I haven't heard any major complaints, so all must be fine." Second, since you may be working on implementation with a group or team, it helps if all members understand the process of action-research and how it applies to program implementation so all can contribute to the process.

The action-research process usually involves the following eight steps:

1. Define target areas for change.
2. Clarify the current situation to hone in on outcome goals.
3. Brainstorm various ways to achieve these outcomes.

4. Weigh the costs and benefits of each option.

5. Choose the options that will most likely lead to your goals.

6. Plan a pilot project to test out your options in detail.

7. Implement with care: emphasize training, carry out the effort with integrity, and monitor the implementation effort.

8. Attend to the outcomes of your efforts.

Action-research is discussed as a cycle; after Step 8, you will be left with a new situation to be clarified (Step 2), and plans for further improvement to be laid. In this way, the action-research process becomes an ongoing and systematic approach in which program implementation and ongoing program modification and improvement come together in what can be referred to as "the spirit of continuous improvement."

Does that sound familiar? As you worked your way through this book, you may have noticed how the action-research process is embedded in the programming approach used. If you have already done Step 1, then you have targeted the area of character education and social-emotional learning. To clarify the situation in your school, you will further specify an area for improvement (perhaps the way staff members model skills, or the way students learn specific social and emotional skills, or the way discipline and crises are handled). Your planning and implementation strategies will bring with them new, challenging situations to be evaluated through the same process. Perhaps in targeting classroom-based instruction and planning and implementing a strategy for it, you realize there are difficulties posed by block scheduling or departmentalized instruction. The action-research process suggests you adapt your initial strategy to address this newly recognized situation.

When should you do assessment? When does the process end? There are no set answers to these questions. You and your staff can plan the schedule of assessment, evaluation, and feedback according to the rule "often enough to be meaningful, but not so often as to be intrusive." The action-research process can even be applied to this decision. One of the items for discussion could be whether the team needs more, less, or different data for its deliberations. Different types of assessment can take place on different schedules (e.g., formal evaluation at certain intervals, less formal feedback at others).

Another important use for action-research is to determine if all relevant groups are benefiting equally from a particular program. Perhaps boys are responding better than girls are, or members of one ethnic group are gaining more than others, or students with special needs are not connecting with the material adequately. If and when you find such disparities, you must modify the program to try to increase the percentage of children you are reaching.

A decision about when to formally "end" the process becomes more a matter of determining what to keep track of, and how intensively, in any given year. Having some kind of feedback system lets students, staff, and others know that you value the initiative and you are concerned with the quality of the effort at all times.

Appendix D

Resources for Social-Emotional Learning and Character Education

The following selected references and resources are included to help with your exploration of social-emotional learning and character education themes and programs. The list of resources is ever growing, and the Internet resources listed will serve as the best gateway to the latest information. Please note that the reference section of this book provides wonderful resources for educators. Several are highlighted here, along with some additional resources.

Books and Manuscripts

Ciarrochi, J., Forgas, J. P., & Mayer, J. D. (2001). *Emotional intelligence in everyday life: A scientific inquiry.* Philadelphia: Psychology Press.

Cohen, J. (Ed.). (1999). *Educating minds and hearts: Social emotional learning and the passage into adolescence.* New York: Teachers College Press.

Cohen, J. (Ed.). (2001). *Caring classrooms/intelligent schools: The social emotional education of young children.* New York: Teachers College Press.

Elias, M. J., Zins, J. E., Weissberg, R. P., Frey, K. S., Greenberg, M. T., Haynes, N. M., Kessler, R., Schwab-Stone, M. E., & Shriver, T. P. (1997). *Promoting social and emotional learning: Guidelines for educators.* Alexandria, VA: Association for Supervision and Curriculum Development.

Goleman, D. (1995). *Emotional intelligence: Why it can matter more than IQ.* New York: Bantam Books.

Graham, J. (1999). It's Up to Us: Giraffe Heroes Program for High School. Langley, WA: Giraffe Project.

Lantieri, L., & Patti, J. (1996). *Waging peace in our schools.* Boston: Beacon Press.

Lions-Quest International. (1998). *Skills for Action.* Baltimore, MD: Quest International.

Scherer, M. (Ed.). Social and Emotional Learning. [Special Issue]. (1997). *Educational Leadership.* 54 (8).

Media

Note: A variety of media resources are available through http://www.casel.org, http://www.nprinc.com, and http://www.communitiesofhope.org. We also suggest the following videos:

- *The Doctor Is In: Emotional Intelligence in the Schools.* Produced by The Dartmouth-Hitchcock Medical Center, One Medical Center Drive, Lebanon, NH 03756 or call 603-643-7400.
- National Center for Innovation and Education (1999). *Lessons for Life: How smart schools boost academic, social, and emotional intelligence.* Bloomington, IN: HOPE Foundation (http://www.communitiesofhope.org).

Via The Internet

- Center for Social and Emotional Education: http://www.csee.net
- Character Education Partnership: http://www.character.org
- Collaboration for Academic, Social, and Emotional Learning: http://www.casel.org
- Lions-Quest International: http://www.quest.edu.
- George Lucas Educational Foundation: http://www.glef.org
- Giraffe Heroes Program:http://www.giraffe.org/k12.htm
- Social Decision Making/Social Problem Solving Program: http://www.umdnj.edu/spsweb

References

Bronfenbrenner, U. (1979). *The ecology of human development: Experiments by nature and design.* Harvard University Press, Cambridge, MA.

Brown, A. & Dowling, P. (1998). *Doing research/reading research: A mode of interrogation for educators.* London: Falmer Press.

Caine, R. N., & Caine, G. (1997). *Education on the edge of possibility.* Alexandria, VA: Association for Supervision and Curriculum Development.

Clabby, J. F. & Elias, M. J. (1986). *Teach your child decision making: An effective 8-step program for parents to teach children to solve everyday problems and make sound decisions.* Garden City, NY: Doubleday.

Deal, T. E., & Kennedy, A. A. (1982). *Corporate cultures: The rite and rituals of corporate life.* Reading, MA: Addison-Wesley.

Elias, M. J. (Ed.) (1993). *Social decision making and life skills development: Guidelines for middle school educators.* Gaithersburg, MD: Aspen.

Elias, M. J., & Clabby, J. F. (1989). *Social decision making skills: A curriculum for the elementary grades.* New Brunswick, NJ: Rutgers University Center for Applied Psychology.

Elias, M. J. & Tobias, S. E. (1996). *Social problem solving interventions in the schools.* New York: The Guilford Press.

Elias, M. J., Tobias, S. E., & Friedlander, B. S. (1999). *Emotionally intelligent parenting.* New York: Harmony Books.

Elias, M. J., Tobias, S. E., & Friedlander, B. S. (2000). *Raising emotionally intelligent teenagers: Parenting with love, laughter, and limits.* New York: Harmony Books.

Elias, M. J., Zins, J. E., Weissberg, R. P., Frey, K. S., Greenberg, M. T., Haynes, N. M., Kessler, R., Schwab-Stone, M. E., & Shriver, T. P. (1997). *Promoting social and emotional learning: Guidelines for educators.* Alexandria, VA: Association for Supervision and Curriculum Development.

Ekman, P., & Davidson, R. J. (1994). *The nature of emotion: Fundamental questions.* New York: Oxford University Press.

Farmer, D. (1999). *National schools of character: Best practices and new perspectives.* Washington, D.C.: Character Education Partnership.

Gardner, H. (1983/1993). *Frames of mind.* New York: Basic Books.

Goleman, D. (1995). *Emotional intelligence: Why it can matter more than IQ.* New York: Bantam Books.

Goleman, D. (1998). *Working with emotional intelligence.* New York: Bantam Books.

Gresham, F. M. and Elliott, S. N. (1990). *Social Skills Rating System Manual.* Minneapolis: American Guidance Service.

Hightower, A. D., Work, W. C., Cowen, E. L., Lotyczewski, B. S., Spinell, A. P., Guare, J. C., & Rohrbeck, C. A. (1986). The Teacher-Child Rating Scale: A brief objective measure of elementary children's school problem behaviors and competencies. *School Psychology Review, 15,* 393-409.

Hord, S. M., Rutherford, W. L., Huling-Austin L., & Hall, G. E. (1987). *Taking charge of change.* Alexandria, VA: Association for Supervision and Curriculum Development.

Jung, C., Pino, R., & Emory, R. (1973). *Research utilizing problem solving: Administrators version.* Leaders Manual. Portland, OR: Northwest Regional Education Laboratory.

Lazarus, R. S. (1999). *Stress and emotion: A new synthesis.* New York: Springer.

Lickona, T., Schaps, E., & Lewis, C. *Eleven principles of effective character education.* Available from the Character Education Partnership, www.character.org. Accessed April 2, 2002.

Maslow, A. H. (1968/1982). *Towards a psychology of being.* New York: Van Nostrand Reinhold.

National Center for Innovation and Education (1999). *Lessons for life: How smart schools boost academic, social, and emotional intelligence.* Bloomington, IN: HOPE Foundation.

Salovey, P., & Sluyter, D. J. (Eds.). (1997). *Emotional development and emotional intelligence: Educational implications.* New York: Basic Books.

Scherer, M. (Ed.) (1997). Social and Emotional Learning [Special Issue]. *Educational Leadership 54* (8).

Schwahn, C., & Spady, W. (1998). Why change doesn't happen and how to make sure it does. *Educational Leadership, 15* (7), 45-47.

Senge, P. (1990). *The fifth discipline: The art and practice of the learning organization*. New York: Doubleday/Currency.

Senge, P., Cambron-McCabe, N., Lucas, T., Smith, B., Dutton, J., & Kleiner, A. (2000). *Schools that learn: A fifth discipline fieldbook for educators, parents, and everyone else who cares about education*. New York: Doubleday.

Spivack, G., & Shure, M. B. (1974). *Social adjustment of young children: A cognitive approach to solving real-life problems*. San Francisco: Jossey-Bass.

Sylwester, R. (1995). *A celebration of neurons: An educator's guide to the human brain*. Alexandria, VA: Association for Supervision and Curriculum Development.

Tierney, W. G. (2001). Why committees don't work: Creating a structure for change. *Academe, 87* (3), 25-29.

Weissberg, R. P., & Greenberg, M. T. (1997). School and community competence enhancement and prevention programs. In: I. E. Sigel & K. A. Renninger (Vol. Eds.), *Handbook of child psychology: Volume 5 child psychology in practice (5th ed.)*. New York: Wiley.

Wheatley, M. J., & Kellner-Rogers, M. (1996). *A simpler way*. San Francisco: Berrett-Koehler.

Wiggins, G., & McTighe, J. (1998). *Understanding by design*. Alexandria, VA: Association for Supervision and Curriculum Development.

Index

About the Authors

Bernard Novick passed away on June 24, 1999. This book is a culmination of his vision and career.

Dr. Novick most recently was the founder and head of Innovative Educational Systems, where he engaged in educational consultation and leadership development activities in schools, multi-district consortia, and business and industry. He received his Doctorate in Education at Rutgers University in 1982, after earning a Masters in 1955 from New York University, where he majored in Personnel and Guidance Administration and minored in School Psychology. Like many educational leaders, Dr. Novick's résumé did not reflect all that he actually did. Nowhere does it mention the time when he temporarily stepped into the Assistant Superintendency of an urban district in New Jersey to save it. Nowhere does it mention his generosity in working with a local religious school to help its management and organization live up to its heart. Throughout his career, Novick fulfilled the expectations for an outstanding school leader—writing grants to initiate and fund career opportunities and vocational education; improving approaches for the district's guidance programs; undertaking close and intense work with the state department of education; working with teacher inservice programs to improve classroom strategies and performance; developing new concepts and procedures in teacher evaluation; establishing procedures for curriculum development; working with groups of students to improve their attitudes toward school, their peers, and their parents; and much more. Dr. Novick inductively used the principles and practices that we now associate with Total Quality Management and Peter Senge's *Fifth Discipline* work.

Roz Gross, an educator in Woodbridge, New Jersey, worked more closely with Dr. Novick over a longer period of time than just about anyone else. She remembers, "Bernie was a unique educator among the group of administrators and was always on the next page. While the rest of us were still dotting the "*i*'s" and crossing the "*t*'s" for some innovative idea he was introducing to the group, he was onto the next idea. But if we did not grasp the concept quickly, Bernie, with infinite patience, explained it again, always finding a different approach. He displayed excellent examples of what a 'master teacher' should do in every classroom every day."

Jeffrey S. Kress is a Senior Research Assistant at the William Davidson Graduate School of Jewish Education at the Jewish Theological Seminary, New York City, where he is also Assistant Professor of Jewish Education. Kress coordinates the Davidson School's Informal/Communal Education concentration. He received his Doctorate in Clinical Psychology from Rutgers University and completed an internship in Clinical/Community Psychology at the University of Medicine and Dentistry of New Jersey. He has worked as a Program Development Specialist at the Social Decision Making/Social Problem Solving Program at University Behavioral HealthCare and University of Medicine and Dentistry of New Jersey, where he conducted teacher training and consultation for a research-validated social-emotional learning curriculum. Currently, his work focuses on bringing theoretical and methodological innovations from the fields of community, clinical, and developmental psychology into the discussion of Jewish identity and Jewish educational program planning.

In particular, he is interested in applying principles of social-emotional learning to Jewish education. Kress has co-authored articles and chapters on the topics of social-emotional learning, program development, and Jewish identity that have been published in a variety of journals and books, and has presented his work at a number of conferences. Kress hosts a Listserv discussion group on the topic of community psychology and spirituality and religion. He can be contacted at the William Davidson Graduate School of Jewish Education at Jewish Theological Seminary, 3080 Broadway, New York, NY 10027; by telephone at (212) 678-8920; fax (212) 749-9085; or e-mail jekress@jtsa.edu.

Maurice J. Elias is Professor in the Department of Psychology at Rutgers University and Co-Developer of the Social Decision Making/Social Problem Solving Project. This project received the 1988 Lela Rowland Prevention Award from the National Mental Health Association, and was recently named a Model Program by the National Educational Goals Panel as well as a Promising Program by the U.S. Department of Education Expert Panel on Safe, Disciplined, and Drug-Free Schools. Dr. Elias is also Vice-Chair of the Leadership Team of the Collaborative for Academic, Social, and Emotional Learning (CASEL), Chairperson of the Program Committee for the Board of Trustees of the Association for Children of New Jersey, and a Trustee of the Hope Foundation. He is a member of the expert panel that advised the development of the NASP/CECP *Early Warning Signs, Timely Response* book on violence prevention and subsequent materials, and is the author of numerous books and articles on prevention. He is also a regular contributor to *Education Week* and to the annual journal of the NJASCD. Dr. Elias is an approved trainer for the N.J. Department of Education, and has authored a weekly column, "FamilyAccents," in the Sunday *Newark Star-Ledger*. With colleagues at CASEL, Dr. Elias was senior author of *Promoting*

Social and Emotional Learning: Guidelines for Educators, published by ASCD. His other books include *Emotionally Intelligent Parenting: How to Raise a Self-Disciplined, Responsible, and Socially Skilled Child* (in its third printing from Harmony/Random House), *Engaging the Resistant Child Through Computers: A Manual for Social and Emotional Learning* (National Professional Resources), and *Raising Emotionally Intelligent Teenagers: Raising Children to be Compassionate, Committed, and Courageous Adults* (Three Rivers Press/Random House). He and the authors maintain a Web site devoted to parenting at www.EQParenting.com. Dr. Elias is married and the father of two children. He can be contacted at Rutgers University, Department of Psychology, 53 Avenue E, Livingston Campus, Piscataway, NJ 08854-8040; by telephone at (732) 445-2444; fax (732) 445-0036; or on the Web at www.EQParenting.com.

Related ASCD Resources
Building Learning Communities with Character: How to Integrate Academic, Social, and Emotional Learning

At the time of publication, the following ASCD resources were available; for the most up-to-date information about ASCD resources, go to www.ascd.org. ASCD stock numbers are noted in parentheses.

Audiotapes

Building Positive Relationships by Reframing Attitudes: The Foundations of Emotional Learning by Sandi Redenbach (#299058)

Emotional Intelligence: A New Model for Curriculum Development by Daniel Goleman (#297100)

Emotional Intelligence and Standards: The Balancing Act by Pam Robbins (#200073)

Introducing a New Educator's Guide to Programs That Promote Students' Social and Emotional Development by Patricia A. Graczyk, Linda Lantieri, John W. Payton, & Roger P. Weissberg (#201173)

Success for Life: Developing a Schoolwide, Curriculum Based Program in Social Emotional Education by Raymond Pasi (#297109)

Teaching Social Skills to Offset Violence in Schools and Communities by Rhonda Buford & Rita Combs-Richardson (#299148)

When Cognitive, Social, Emotional, and Moral Development Converge by Don Murk & Keith Pentz (#200205)

Multimedia

Emotional Intelligence Professional Inquiry Kit by Pam Robbins (#997146)

Networks

Visit the ASCD Web site (www.ascd.org) and search for "networks" for information about professional educators who have formed groups around topics like "Character Education," "Service Learning/Experimental Learning (SELNET)," "Invitational Education," and "Mentoring Leadership and Resources." Look in the "Network Directory" for current facilitators' addresses and phone numbers.

Online Resources

Visit ASCD's Web site (www.ascd.org) for the following professional development opportunities:

Educational Leadership: Social and Emotional Learning (entire issue, May 1997). Excerpted articles online free (http://www.ascd.org /frameedlead.html); entire issue online and accessible to ASCD members (http://www.ascd.org/membersonly.html)

Online Tutorials: *Character Education,* among others (http://www.ascd.org/frametutorials .html) (free)

Professional Development Online: *Classroom Management: Building Relationships for Better Learning,* among others (http://www.ascd.org/framepdonline.html) (for a small fee; password protected)

Print Products

Connecting Character to Conduct: Helping Students Do the Right Things by Rita Stein, Roberta Richin, Richard Banyon, Francine Banyon, & Marc Stein (#100209)

Educating Minds and Hearts: Social Emotional Learning and the Passage into Adolescence edited by Jonathan Cohen (#199001)

Every Child Learning: Safe and Supportive Schools by the Learning First Alliance (#301279)

Promoting Social and Emotional Learning: Guidelines for Educators by Maurice J. Elias, Joseph E. Zins, Roger P. Weissberg, Karin S. Frey, Mark T. Greenberg, Norris M. Haynes, Rachael Kessler, Mary E. Schwab-Stone, & Timothy P. Shriver (#197157)

The Soul of Education: Helping Students Find Connection, Compassion, and Character at School by Rachael Kessler (#100045)

Teaching Conflict Resolution with the Rainbow Kids Program by Barbara Porro (#101247)

For more information, visit us on the World Wide Web (http://www.ascd.org), send an e-mail message to member@ascd.org, call the ASCD Service Center (1-800-933-ASCD or 703-578-9600, then press 2), send a fax to 703-575-5400, or write to Information Services, ASCD, 1703 N. Beauregard St., Alexandria, VA 22311-1714 USA.